Helen Hunt Jackson

Hetty's Strange History

Helen Hunt Jackson

Hetty's Strange History

ISBN/EAN: 9783743399631

Manufactured in Europe, USA, Canada, Australia, Japa

Cover: Foto ©ninafisch / pixelio.de

Manufactured and distributed by brebook publishing software (www.brebook.com)

Helen Hunt Jackson

Hetty's Strange History

NO NAME SERIES.

HETTY'S STRANGE HISTORY.

NO NAME SERIES.

"Is the Gentleman anonymous? Is he a Great Unknown?"
DANIEL DERONDA.

HETTY'S STRANGE HISTORY.

BY THE
AUTHOR OF "MERCY PHILBRICK'S CHOICE."

BOSTON:
ROBERTS BROTHERS.
1877.

Copyright, 1877,
By Roberts Brothers.

What lover best his love doth prove and show?
The one whose words are swiftest, love to state?
The one who measures out his love by weight
In costly gifts which all men see and know?
Nay! words are cheap and easy: they may go
For what men think them worth: or soon or late,
They are but air. And gifts? Still cheaper rate
Are they at which men barter to and fro
Where love is not!
     One thing remains. Oh, Love,
Thou hast so seldom seen it on the earth,
No name for it has ever sprung to birth;
To give one's own life up one's love to prove,
Not in the martyr's death, but in the dearth
Of daily life's most wearing daily groove.

II.

And unto him who this great thing hath done,
What does Great Love return? No speedy joy!
That swift delight which beareth large alloy
Is guerdon Love bestowed on him who won
A lesser trust: the happiness begun
In happiness, of happiness may cloy,
And, its own subtle foe, itself destroy.
But steadfast, tireless, quenchless as the sun
Doth grow that gladness which hath root in pain.
Earth's common griefs assail this soul in vain.
Great Love himself, too poor to pay such debt,
Doth borrow God's great peace which passeth yet
All understanding. Full tenfold again
Is found the life, laid down without regret!

1597025

HETTY'S STRANGE HISTORY.

I.

WHEN Squire Gunn and his wife died, within three months of each other, and Hetty their only child was left alone in the big farm-house, everybody said, "Well, now Hetty Gunn 'll have to make up her mind to marry somebody." And it certainly looked as if she must. What could be lonelier than the position of a woman thirty-five years of age sole possessor of a great stone house, half a dozen barns and out-buildings, herds of cattle, and a farm of five hundred acres? The place was known as "Gunn's," far and wide. It had been a rich and prosperous farm ever since the days of the first Squire Gunn, Hetty's grandfather. He was one of Massachusetts' earliest militia-men, and had a leg shot off at Lexington. To the old man's dying day he used to grow red in the face whenever he told the story, and bring his fist down hard on the table, with "Damn the leg, sir! 'Twasn't the leg I cared for: 'twas the not having another chance at those damned British rascals;" and the wooden leg itself would twitch and rap on the floor in his impatient indignation. One of Hetty's earliest recollections was of being led about the farm by this warm-hearted, irascible, old grandfather, whose wooden leg was a perpetual and unfathomable mystery to her. Where the flesh leg left off and the wooden leg began, and if, when the wooden leg stumped so loud and hard on the floor, it did not hurt the flesh leg at the other end, puzzled little Hetty's head for many a long hour. Her grandfather's frequent and comic references to the honest old wooden pin did not diminish her perplexities. He was something of a wag, the old Squire; and nothing came handier to him, in the way of a joke, than a joke at his own expense. When he was eighty years old, he had a stroke of paralysis: he lived six years after that; but he could not walk about the farm any longer. He used to sit in a big cane-bottomed chair close to the fireplace, in winter, and under a big lilac-bush, at the north-east corner of the house, in summer. He kept a stout iron-tipped cane by his side: in the winter, he used it to poke the fire with; in the summer, to rap the hens and chickens which he used to lure round his chair by handfuls of corn and oats. Sometimes he would tap the end of the wooden leg with this cane, and say, laughingly, " Ha! ha! think of a leg like that's being paralyzed, if you please. Isn't that a joke? It's just as paralyzed as the other: damn those British rascals." And only a few hours before he died, he said to his son: " Look here, Abe, you put on my grave-stone, —'Here lies Abraham Gunn, all but one leg.' What do you suppose one-legged men're going to do in the resurrection, hey, Abe? I'll ask the parson if he comes in this afternoon," he added. But, when the parson came, the brave, merry eyes were shut for ever, and the old hero had gone to a new world, on which he no doubt entered as resolutely and cheerily as he had gone through nearly a century of this. These glimpses of the old Squire's characteristics are not out of place here, although he himself has no place in our story, having been dead and buried for more than twenty years before the story begins. But he lived again in his granddaughter Hetty. How much of her offhand, comic, sturdy, resolute, disinterested nature came to her by direct inheritance from his blood, and how much was absorbed as she might have absorbed it from any one she loved and associated with, it is impossible to tell. But by one process or the other, or by both, Hetty Gunn was, as all the country people round about said, "Just the old Squire over again," and if they sometimes added, as it must be owned they did, "It's a thousand pities she wasn't a boy," there was, in this reflection on the Creator, no reflection on Hetty's womanliness: it was rather on the accepted theory and sphere of woman's activities and manifestations. Nobody in this world could have a tenderer heart than Hetty: this also she had inherited or learned from her grandfather. Many a day the two had spent together in nursing a sick or maimed chicken, or a half-frozen lamb, even a woodchuck that had got its leg broken in a trap was not an outcast to them; and as for beggars and tramps, not one passed "Gunn's," from June till October, that was not hailed by the old squire from under his lilac-bush, and fed by Hetty. Plenty of sarcastic and wholesome advice the old gentleman gave them, while they sat on the ground eating; and every word of it sank into Hetty's wide-open ears and sensible soul, developing in her a very rare sort of thing which, for want of a better name, we might call common-sense sympathy. To this sturdy common-sense barrier against the sentimental side of sympathy with other people's sufferings, Hetty added an equally sturdy, and she would have said common-sense, fortitude in bearing her own. This invaluable trait she owed largely to her grandfather's wooden leg. Before she could speak plain, she had already made his cheerful way of bearing the discomfort and annoyance of that queer leg her own standard of patience and equanimity. Nothing that ever happened to her, no pain, no deprivation, seemed half so dreadful as a wooden leg. She used to stretch out her own fat, chubby, little legs, and look from them to her grandfather's. Then she would timidly touch the wooden tip which rested on the floor, and look up in her grandfather's face, and say, "Poor Grandpa!"

"Pshaw! pshaw! child," he would reply, "that's nothing. It does almost as well to walk on, and that's all legs are for. I'd have had forty legs shot off rather than not have helped drive out those damned British rascals."

Not even for sake of Hetty's young ears could the old Squire mention the British rascals without his favorite expletive. Here, also, came in another lesson which sank deep into Hetty's heart. It was for his country that her grandfather had lost that leg, and would have gladly lost forty, if he had had so many to lose, not for himself; for something which he loved better than himself: this was distinct in Hetty Gunn's comprehension before she was twelve years old, and it was a most important force in the growth of her nature. No one can estimate the results on a character of these slow absorptions, these unconscious biases, from daily contact. All precepts, all religions, are insignificant agencies by their side. They are like sun and soil to a plant: they make a moral climate in which certain things are sure to grow, and certain other things are sure to die; as sure as it is that orchids and pineapples thrive in the tropics, and would die in New England.

When old Squire Gunn was buried, all the villages within twenty miles turned out to his funeral. He was the last revolutionary hero of the county. An oration was delivered in the meeting-house; and the brass band of Welbury played "My country, 'tis of thee," all the way from the meeting-house to the graveyard gate. After the grave was filled up, guns were fired above it, and the Welbury village choir sang an anthem. The crowd, the music, the firing of guns, produced an ineffaceable impression upon Hetty's mind. While her grandfather's body lay in the house, she had wept inconsolably. But as soon as the funeral services began, her tears stopped; her eyes grew large and bright with excitement; she held her head erect; a noble exaltation and pride shone on her features; she gazed upon the faces of the people with a composure and dignity which were unchildlike. No emperor's daughter in Rome could have borne herself, at the burial of her most illustrious ancestor, more grandly and yet more modestly than did little Hetty Gunn, aged twelve, at the burial of this unfamed Massachusetts revolutionary soldier: and well she might; for a greater than royal inheritance had come to her from him. The echoes of the farewell shots which were fired over the old man's grave were never to die out of Hetty's ears. Child, girl, woman, she was to hear them always: signal guns of her life, they meant courage, cheerfulness, self-sacrifice.

Of Hetty's father, the "young Squire," as to the day of his death he was called by the older people in Welbury, and of Hetty's mother, his wife, it is not needful to say much here. The young Squire was a lazy, affectionate man to whom the good things of life had come without his taking any trouble for them: even his wife had been more than half wooed for him by his doting father; and there were those who said that pretty Mrs. Gunn had been quite as much in love with the old Squire, old as he was, as with the young one; but that was only an idle village sneer. The young Squire and his wife loved each other devotedly, and their only child, Hetty, with an unreasoning and unreasonable affection which would have been the ruin of her, if she had been any thing else but what she was, "the old Squire over again." As it was, the only effect of this overweening affection, on their part, was to produce a slow reversal of some of the ordinary relations between parents and children. As Hetty grew into womanhood, she grew more and more to have a sense of responsibility for her father's and mother's happiness. She was the most filially docile of creatures, and obeyed like a baby, grown woman as she was. It was strange to hear and to see.

"Hetty, bring me my overcoat," her father would say to her in her thirty-fifth year, exactly as he would have said it in her twelfth; and she would spring with the same alacrity and the same look of pleasure at being of use. But there was a filial service which she rendered to her parents much deeper than these surface obediences and attentions. They were but dimly conscious of it; and yet, had it been taken away from them, they had found their lives blighted indeed. She was the link between them and the outside world. She brought merriment, cheer, hearty friendliness into the house. She was the good comrade of every young woman and every young man in Welbury; and she compelled them all to bring a certain halffilial affection and attention to her father and mother. The best tribute to what she had accomplished in this direction was in the fact, that you always heard the young people mention Squire Gunn and his wife as "Hetty Gunn's father" or "Hetty Gunn's mother;" and the two old people were seen at many a gathering where there was not a single old face but theirs.

"Hetty won't go without her father and mother," or "Hetty 'll be so pleased if we ask her father and mother," was frequently heard. From this free and unembarrassed association of the old and the young, grew many excellent things. In this wholesome atmosphere honesty and good behavior thrived; but there was little chance for the development of those secret sentimental preferences and susceptibilities out of which spring love-making and thoughts of marriage.

There probably was not a marriageable young man in Welbury who had not at one time or another thought to himself, what a good thing it would be to marry Hetty Gunn. Hetty was pretty, sensible, affectionate, and rich. Such girls as that were not to be found every day. A man might look far and long before he could find such a wife as Hetty would make. But nothing seemed to be farther from Hetty's thoughts than making a wife of herself for anybody. And the world may say what it pleases about its being the exclusive province of men to woo: very few men do woo a woman who does not show herself ready to be wooed. It is a rare beauty or a rare spell of some sort which can draw a man past the barrier of a woman's honest, unaffected, and persistent unconsciousness of any thoughts of love or matrimony. So between Hetty's unconsciousness and her perpetual comradeship with her father and mother, the years went on, and on, and no man asked Hetty to marry him. The odd thing about it was that every man felt sure that he was the only man who had not asked her; and a general impression had grown up in the town that Hetty Gunn had refused nearly everybody. She was so evidently a favorite; "Gunn's" was so much the headquarters for all the young people; it was so open to everybody's observation how much all men admired and liked Hetty, — she was never seen anywhere without one or two or three at her service: it was the most natural thing in the world for people to think as they did. Yet not a human being ever accused Hetty of flirting; her manner was always as open, friendly, and cordial as an honest boy's, and with no more trace of self-seeking or self-consciousness about it. She was as full of fun and mischief, too, as any boy could be. She had slid down hill with the wildest of them, till even her father said sternly, —

"Hetty, — you're too big. It's a shameful sight to see a girl of your size, out on a sled with boys." And Hetty hung her head, and said pathetically, —

"I wish I hadn't grown. I'd rather be a dwarf, than not slide down hill."

But after the sliding was forbidden, there remained the chestnuttings in the autumn, and the trout fishings in the summer, and the Mayflower parties in the spring, and colts and horses and dogs. Until Hetty was twenty-two years old, you might have been quite sure that, whenever you found her in any out-door party, the masculine element was largely predominant in that party. After this time, however, life gradually sobered for Hetty: one by one her friends married; the maidens became matrons, the young men became heads of houses. In wedding after wedding, Hetty Gunn was the prettiest of the bridesmaids, and people whispered as they watched her merry, kindly face, —

"Ain't it the queerest thing in life, Hetty Gunn won't marry. There isn't a fellow in town she mightn't have."

If anybody had said this to Hetty herself, she would probably have laughed, and said with entire frankness, —

"You're quite mistaken. They don't want me," which would only have strengthened her hearers' previous impressions that they did.

In process of time, after the weddings came the christenings, and at these also Hetty Gunn was still the favorite friend, the desired guest. Presently, there came to be so many little Hetty Gunns in the village, that no young mother had courage to use the name more, however much she loved Hetty. Hetty used to say laughingly that it was well she was an only child, for she had now more nieces and nephews than she knew what to do with. Very dearly she loved them all; and the little things all loved her, the instant she put her arms round them: and more than one young husband, without meaning to be in the least disloyal to his wife, thought to himself, when he saw his baby's face nestling down to Hetty Gunn's brown curls, —

"I wonder if she'd have had me, if I'd asked her. But I don't believe Hetty'll ever marry, — a girl that's had the offers she has."

And so it had come to pass that, at the time our story begins, Hetty was thirty-five years old, and singularly alone in the world. The death of her mother, which had occurred first, was a great shock to her, for it had been a sudden and a painful death. But the loss of her mother was to Hetty a trivial one, in comparison with the loss of her father. On the day of her grandfather's death, she had seemed, child as she was, to have received her father into her hands, as a sacred legacy of trust; and he, on his part, seemed fully to reciprocate and accept without comprehending the new relation. He unconsciously leaned upon Hetty more and more from that hour until the hour when he died, bolstered up in bed with his head on her shoulder, and gasping out, between difficult breaths, his words of farewell,—strange farewell to be spoken to a middle-aged woman, whose hair was already streaked with gray,—

"Poor little girl! I've got to leave you. You've been a good little girl, Hetty, a good little girl."

Neighbors and friends crowded around Hetty, in the first moments of her grief. But they all, even those nearest and most intimate, found themselves bewildered and baffled, nay almost repelled, by Hetty's manner. Her noble face was so grief-stricken that she looked years older in a single day. But her voice and her smile were unaltered; and she would not listen to any words of sympathy. She wished to hear no allusions to her trouble, except such as were needfully made in the arranging of practical points. Her eyes filled with tears frequently, but no one saw a tear fall. At the funeral, her face wore much the same look it had worn, twenty-three years before, at her grandfather's funeral. There were some present who remembered that day well, and remembered the look, and they said musingly,—

"There's something very queer about Hetty Gunn, after all. Don't you remember how she acted, when she was a little thing, the day old Squire Gunn was buried? Anybody 'd have thought then a funeral was Fourth of July, and she looks much the same way now."

Then they fell to discussing the probabilities of her future course. It was not easy to predict.

"The Squire's left every thing to her, just as if she was a man. She can sell the property right off, if she wants to, and go and live where she likes," they said.

"Well, you may set your minds to rest on that," said old Deacon Little, who had been the young squire's most intimate friend, and who knew Hetty as well as if she were his own child, and loved her better; for his own children, poor man, had nearly brought his gray hairs down to the grave with distress and shame.

"Hetty Gunn 'll never sell that farm, not a stick nor a stone on't, any more than the old Squire himself would. You 'll see, she 'll keep it a goin', jest the same 's ever. It's a thousand pities, she warn't born a boy."

II.

THE funeral took place late in the afternoon of a warm April day. The roads were very muddy, and the long procession wound back to the village about as slowly as it had gone out. One by one, wagon after wagon fell out of the line, and turned off to the right or left, until there were left only the Gunns' big carryall, in which sat Hetty, with her two house-servants, — an old black man and his wife, who had been in her father's house so long, that their original patronymic had fallen entirely out of use, and they were known as "Cæsar Gunn" and "Nan Gunn" the town over. Behind this followed their farm wagon, in which sat the farmer and his wife with their babies, and the two farm laborers, — all Irish, and all crying audibly after the fashion of their race. As they turned into the long avenue of pines which led up to the house, their grief broke out louder and louder; and, when the wagon stopped in front of the western piazza, their sobs and cries became howls and shrieks. Hetty, who was just entering the front-door, turned suddenly, and walking swiftly toward them, said, in a clear firm tone, —

"Look here! Mike, Dan, Norah, I'm ashamed of you. Don't you see you're frightening the poor little children? Be quiet. The one who loved my father most will be the first one to go about his work as if nothing had happened. Mike, saddle the pony for me at six. I am going to ride over to Deacon Little's."

The men were too astonished to reply, but gazed at her dumbly. Mike muttered sullenly, as he drove on, —

"An' it's a quare way to be showin' our love, I'm thinkin'."

"An' it's Miss Hetty's own way thin, by Jasus!" answered Dan; "an' I'd jist loike to see the man 'ud say, she didn't fairly worship the very futsteps of 'im."

When Deacon Little heard Hetty Gunn's voice at his door that night, the old man sprang to his feet as he had not sprung for twenty years.

"Bless my soul!" he exclaimed, "what can have brought Hetty Gunn here to-night?" and he met her in the hall with outstretched hands.

"Hetty, my dear, what is it?" he exclaimed, in a tone of anxiety.

"Oh!" said Hetty, earnestly. "I have frightened you, haven't I? was it wrong for me to come to-night? There are so many things I want to talk over with you. I want to get settled; and all the work on the farm is belated: and I can't have the place run behindhand; that would worry father so."

The tears stood in her eyes, but she spoke in as matter-of-course a tone as if she had simply come as her father's messenger to ask advice. The old deacon pushed his spectacles high upon his forehead, and, throwing his head back, looked at Hetty a moment, scrutinizingly, in silence. Then, he said, half to himself, half to her, —

"You're your grandfather all over, Hetty. Now let me know what I can help you about. You can always come to me, as long as I'm alive, Hetty. You know that."

"Yes," said Hetty, walking back and forth in the little room, rapidly. "You are the only person I shall ever ask any thing of in that way."

"Sit down, Hetty, sit down," said the old man. "You must be all worn out."

"Oh, no! I'm not tired: I was never tired in my life," replied Hetty. "Let me walk: it does me good to walk; I walked nearly all last night;

it seems to be something to do. You see, Mr. Little," she said,—pausing suddenly, and folding her arms on her breast, as she looked at him,—"I don't quite see my way clear yet; and one must see one's way clear before one can be quiet. It's horrible to grope."

"Yes, yes, child," said the deacon, hesitatingly. He did not understand metaphor. "You are not thinking of going away, are you, Hetty?"

"Going away!" exclaimed Hetty. "Why, what do you mean? How could I go away? Besides, I wouldn't go for any thing in the world. What should I go away for?"

"Well, I'm real glad to hear you say so, Hetty," replied the deacon warmly; "some folks have said, you'd most likely sell the farm, and go away."

"What fools! I'd as soon sell myself," said Hetty, curtly. "But I can't live there all alone. And one thing I wanted to ask you about to-night was, whether you thought it would do for your James and his wife to come and live there with me: I would give him a good salary as a sort of overseer. Of course, I should expect to control every thing; and that's not much more than I have done for three or four years: but the men will do better with a man to give them their orders, than they will with me alone. I could do this better with Jim than I could with a stranger. I've always liked Jim."

Deacon Little did not reply. His eyes were fixed on the ground, and his face flushed with agitation. At last he said huskily, —

"Would you really take Jim and Sally home to your house, to live with you, Hetty?"

"Why, certainly," replied Hetty, in an impatient tone, "that's what I said: didn't I make it plain?" and she walked faster and faster back and forth.

"Hetty, you're an angel," exclaimed the old man, solemnly. "If there's any thing that could make him hold up his head again, it would be just that thing. "But — " he hesitated, "you know Sally?"

"Yes, yes, I know her. I know all about her. She's a poor, weak thing," said Hetty, with no shade of tenderness in her voice; "but Jim was the most to blame, and it's abominable the way people have treated her. I always wished I could do something for them both, and now I've got the chance: that is if you think they'd like to come."

The deacon hesitated again, began to speak, broke off, hesitated, tried again, and at last stammered : —

"Don't think I don't feel your kindness, Hetty; but, low's Jim's fallen, I don't quite feel like having them go into anybody's kitchen, especially with black help."

"Kitchen!" interrupted Hetty. "What do you take me for, Deacon Little? If Jim comes to live with me as my overseer, he is just the same as my partner in the place, so far as his position goes. How do you suppose I thought that the men would respect him, and take orders from him, if I meant to put him in the kitchen with Cæsar and Nan? No indeed, they shall live with me as if they were my brother and sister. There are plenty of rooms in the house for them to have their own sitting-room, and be by themselves as much as they like. Kitchen indeed! I think you've forgotten that Jim and I were schoolmates from the time we were six till we were twenty. I always liked Jim, and he hasn't had half a chance yet: that miserable affair pulled him down when he was so young."

"That's so, Hetty; that's so," said the deacon, with tears rolling down his wrinkled cheeks. "Jim wasn't a bad boy. He never meant to harm anybody, and he hasn't had any chance at all since that happened. It seems as if it took all the spirit right out of him; and Sally, she hasn't got any spirit either: she's been nothin' but a millstone round his neck. It's a mercy the baby died: that's one thing."

"I don't think so at all, Mr. Little," said Hetty, vehemently. "I think if the baby had lived, it would have strengthened them both. It would have made Sally much happier, at any rate. She is a motherly little thing."

"Yes," said the old man, reluctantly. "Sally's affectionate; I won't deny that: but"—and an expression of exceeding bitterness passed over his face—"I wish to the Lord I needn't ever lay my eyes on her face again! I can't feel right towards her, and I don't suppose I ever shall."

"I wouldn't wonder if the time came when she was a real comfort to you, Mr. Little," said Hetty, cheerily. "You get them to come and live with me and see what that'll do. I can afford to give Jim more than he can make at surveying. I have a notion he's a better farmer than he is engineer, isn't he?"

"Yes, there's nothing Jim don't know about a farm. I always did hope he'd settle down here at home with us. But we couldn't have Sally in the house: it would have killed Mrs. Little.

It gives her a day's nervous headache now, long ago's 'tis, whenever she sees her on the street."

"Well, well," said Hetty, impatiently, "she won't give anybody nervous headaches in my house, poor little soul, that's certain; and the sooner they can come the better I shall like it. So you will arrange it all for me at once, won't you?"

Then Hetty went on to speak of some matters in regard to the farm about which she was in doubt,—as to certain fields, and crops, and what should be done with the young stock from last year. Presently the old clock in the hall struck nine, and the village bells began to ring.

Hetty sprang to her feet.

"Dear me!" she exclaimed, "I had no idea it was so late. I only meant to stay an hour. Nan will be frightened about me." And she was out of the house and on her pony's back almost before Deacon Little could say,—

"But, Hetty, ain't you afraid to go home by yourself. I can go with you's well's not."

"Bless me, no!" said Hetty. "I always ride alone. Polly knows the road as well as I do;" and she cantered off, saying cheerily, "Good-night, deacon, I can't tell you how much I'm obliged to you. Please see Jim's early's you can to-morrow: I want to get settled and begin work."

When Hetty reached home, the house was silent and dark: only one feeble light glimmered in the hall. As she threw open the door, old Cæsar and Nan rushed forward together from the kitchen, exclaiming, half sobbing,—

"Oh, Miss Hetty! Miss Hetty! we made sure you was killed."

"Nonsense, Nan!" said Hetty, goodnaturedly: "what put such an idea into your head? Haven't I ridden Polly many a darker night than this?"

"Yes'm," sobbed Nan; "but to-night's different. All our luck's gone: 'When the master's dead, the house is shook,' they say where I was raised. Oh, Miss Hetty! it's lonesome's death in the kitchen."

Hetty threw open the door into the sitting-room. "Put on a stick of wood, Nan, and make the fire blaze up," she said.

While Nan was doing this, Hetty lighted the lamps, drew down the curtains, and gave the room its ordinary evening look. Then she said,—

"Now, Nan, sit down: I want to talk with

you," and Hetty herself sat down in her father's chair on the right hand of the fireplace.

"Oh, Miss Hetty!" cried Nan, "don't you go set in that chair: you'll die before the year's out if you do. Oh please, Miss Hetty! get right up;" and the poor old woman took forcible hold of her young mistress's arms, and tried to lift her from the chair.

"To please you, I will sit in another chair now, Nan, because I want you to be quiet and listen to me. But that will be my chair to sit in always, just as it used to be my father's; and I shall not die before the year's out, Nan, nor I hope for a great many years to come yet," said Hetty.

"Oh, no! please the Lord, Miss Hetty," sobbed Nan: "who'd take care of Cæsar an' me ef you was to die."

"But I expect you and Cæsar to take care of me, Nan," replied Hetty, smiling, "and I want to have a good talk with you now, and make you understand about our life here. You want to please me, don't you, Nan?"

"Oh, yes! Miss Hetty. You knows I do, and so does Cæsar. We wouldn't have no other missus, not in all these Norf States: we'd sooner go back down where we was raised."

Hetty smiled involuntarily at this violent comparison, knowing well that both Cæsar and Nan would have died sooner than go back to the land where they were "raised." But she went on,—

"Very well. You never need have any other mistress as long as I live: and when I die you and Cæsar will have money enough to make you comfortable, and a nice little house. Now the first thing I want you to understand is that we are going to live on here in this house, exactly as we did when my father was here. I shall carry on the farm exactly as he would if he were alive; that is, as nearly as I can. Now you will make it very hard for me, if you cry and are lonesome, and say such things as you said to-night. If you want to please me, you will go right on with your work cheerfully, and behave just as if your master were sitting there in his chair all the time. That is what will please him best, too, if he is looking on, as I don't doubt he very often will be."

"But is you goin' to be here all alone, Miss Hetty? yer don't know what yer a layin' out for, yer don't," interrupted Nan.

"No," replied Hetty: "Mr. James Little and his wife are coming here to stay. He will be overseer of the farm."

"What! Her that was Sally Newhall?" exclaimed Nan, in a sharp tone.

"Yes, that was Mrs. Little's name before she was married," replied Hetty, looking Nan full in the face with a steady expression, intended to restrain any farther remarks on the subject of Mrs. Little. But Nan was not to be restrained.

"Before she was married! Yes 'm! an' a good deal too late 'twas she was married too. 'Deed, Miss Hetty, yer ain't never going to take her in to live with you, be yer?" she muttered.

"Yes, I am, Nan," Hetty said firmly; "and you must never let such a word as that pass your lips again. You will displease me very much if you do not treat Mrs. Little respectfully."

"But, Miss Hetty," persisted Nan. "Yer don't know"—

"Yes, I do, Nan: I know it all. But I pity them both very much. We have all done wrong in one way or another; and it is the Lord's business to punish people, not ours. You've often told me, Nan, about that pretty little girl of yours and Cæsar's that died when I was a baby. Supposing she had lived to be a woman, and some one had led her to do just as wrong as poor Sally Little did, wouldn't you have thought it very hard if the whole world had turned against her, and never given her a fair chance again to show that she was sorry and meant to live a good life?"

Nan was softened.

"'Deed would I, Miss Hetty. But that don't make me feel like seein' that gal a settin' down to table with you, Miss Hetty, now I tell yer! Cæsar nor me couldn't stand that nohow!"

"Yes you can, Nan; and you will, when you know that it would make me very unhappy to have you be unkind to her," answered Hetty, firmly. "She and her husband both, have done all in their power to atone for their wrong; and nobody has ever said a word against Mrs. Little since her marriage; and one thing I want distinctly understood, Nan, by every one on this place, — any disrespectful word or look towards Mr. or Mrs. Little will be just the same as if it were towards me myself."

Nan was silenced, but her face wore an obstinate expression which gave Hetty some misgivings as to the success of her experiment. However, she knew that Nan could be trusted to repeat to the other servants all that she had said, and that it would lose nothing in the recital; and, as for the future, one of Hetty's first principles of action was an old proverb which her grandfather had explained to her when she was a little girl, —

"Don't cross bridges till you come to them."

III.

THE gratitude with which James Little's wife received Hetty's proposition was so great that it softened even her father-in-law's heart.

"I do believe, Hetty," he said, when he gave her their answer, "I do believe that poor girl has suffered more 'n we 've given her credit for. When I explained to her that you was goin' to take her right in to be like one o' your own family, she turned as white as a sheet, and says she, —

"'You don't mean it, father: she won't ever dare to:' and when I said, says I, —

"'Yes, she does: Hetty Gunn ain't a girl not to know what she means to do. And that's just what she says she's goin' to do with you and Jim,' she broke right out crying, out loud, just like a little baby, and says she, —

"'If the Lord don't bless Hetty Gunn for bein' so good to us! she sha'n't ever be sorry for it's long's she lives.'"

"Of course I sha'n't," said Hetty, bluntly. "I never was sorry yet for any thing I did which was right, and I am as sure this is right as I am that I am alive. When will they come?"

"Sarah said she would come right over to-day, if you'd like to have her help you; and Jim he could fix up things at home, and shut the house up. Jim said they'd better not let the house till you had tried how it worked havin' 'em here. Jim don't seem very sanguine about it. Poor fellow, he's got the spirit all taken out of him."

"Well, well, we'll put it back again, see if we don't, before the year is out," replied Hetty, with a beaming smile, which made her face beautiful.

It happened fortunately that poor Sarah Little first came to her new home alone, rather than with her husband. The years of solitude and disgrace through which they had lived, had made him dogged and defiant of manner, but had made her humble and quiet. She still kept a good deal of the beauty of her youth; and there were few persons who could be unmoved by the upward glance of her saddened blue eyes. In less than five minutes, she conquered old Nan, and secured her as an ally for ever. As she entered the house, Hetty met her, and saying cordially, —

"I'm glad to see you, Sally. It was so good of

you to come right over at once; we have a great deal to do," — she kissed her on her forehead.

Sarah burst into tears. Nan stood by with a sullen face. Turning towards her involuntarily, perhaps because she hardly dared to speak to Hetty, Sarah said, —

"Oh, Nan, I'm only crying because she is so kind to me. I can't help it;" and the poor thing sank into a chair and sobbed. No wonder! it was six years since she had returned to her native village, a shame-stricken woman, bearing in her arms the child whose birth had been her disgrace. That its father was now her husband did little or nothing to repair the loss which her weakness and wrong-doing had entailed on her. If there be a pitiless community in this world, it is a small New England village. Calvinism, in its sternest aspects, broods over it; narrowness and monotony make rigid the hearts which theology has chilled; and a grim Pharisaism, born of a certain sort of intellectual keen-wittedness, completes the cruel inhumanity. It was six years since poor Sarah Little, baby in arms, had come into such an air as this, — six years, and until this moment, when Hetty Gunn kissed her forehead and spoke to her with affection, no woman had ever said to her a kindly word. When the baby died, not a neighbor came to its funeral. The minister, the weeping father and mother, and the stern-looking grandfather, alone followed the little unwelcomed one to its grave. After that, Sarah rarely went out of her house except at night. The tradesmen with whom she had to deal came slowly to have a pitying respect for her. The minister went occasionally to see her, and in his clumsy way thought he perceived what he called "the right spirit" in her. Sarah dreaded his calls more than any thing else. What made her isolation much harder to bear was the fact that, only two years before, every young girl in the county had been her friend. There was no such milliner in all that region as Sarah Newhall. In autumn and in spring, her little shop at Lonway Four Corners was crowded with chattering and eager girls, choosing ribbons and hats, and all deferring to her taste. Now they all passed her by with only a cold and silent bow. Not one spoke. To Sarah's affectionate, mirth-loving temperament, this was misery greater than could be expressed. She said not a word about it, not even to her husband: she bore it as dumb animals bear pain, seeking only a shelter, a hiding-place; but she wished herself dead. Jim's share of the punishment had been in some ways lighter than hers, in others harder. He had less loneliness; but, on the other hand, by his constant intercourse with men, he was freqently reminded of the barrier which separated himself and his wife from all that went on in the village. He had the same mirthful, social temperament which she had: the thoughtless, childish, pleasure-loving quality, which they had in common, had been the root of their sin; and was now the instrument of their suffering. Stronger people could have borne up better; worse people might have found a certain evil solace in evil ways and with evil associates: but Jim and Sally were incapable of any such course; they were simply two utterly broken-spirited and hopeless children whose punishment had been greater than they could bear. In a dogged way, because they must live, Jim went on earning a little money as surveyor and draughtsman. He often talked of going away into some new faraway place where they could have, as he said, in the same words Hetty had used, "a fair chance;" but Sally would not go. "It would not make a bit of difference," she said: "it would be sure to be found out, and strange folks would despise us even more than our own folks do; perhaps things will come round right after a while, if we stay here."

Jim did not insist, for he loved Sally tenderly; and he felt, to the core of his heart, that the least he could do for her now was to let her live where she chose to live: but he grew more sullen and dogged, day by day; and Sally grew sadder and quieter, and things were fast coming to a bad pass, when Hetty Gunn's generous offer came to them, like a great rift of sunlight in a black sky.

When Sally sank into the chair sobbing, Hetty made a quick movement towards her, and was about to speak; but, seeing that old Nan was hastening to do the same thing, she wisely waited, thinking to herself, —

"If Nan will only take her under her wing, all will go well."

Old Nan's tenderness of heart was unlimited. If her worst enemy were in pain or sorrow, she would succor him: ready perhaps to take up the threads of her resentment again, as soon as his sufferings were alleviated; but a very Samaritan of good offices as long as he needed them. Cæsar, so well understood this trait in her, that in their matrimonial disputes, which, it must be confessed, were frequent and sharp, when all other weapons failed him, he fell back on the colic. He had only to interrupt the torrent of her reproaches, with a groan, and a twist of his fat abdomen, and "oh, honey, I'm so bad in my stomach!" and she was transformed, in an instant from a Xantippe into a Florence Nightingale: the whole current of her wrath deviated from him to the last meal he had eaten, whatever it might be.

"Now, it's jist nothin' but that pesky bacon you ate this mornin', Cæsar: you sha'n't never touch a bit again 's long 's you live; do you hear?" and with hot water and flannels, she would proceed to comfort and coddle him as if no anger had ever stirred her heart.

When she saw poor Sarah Little sink crying into a chair, and heard the humble gratefulness of her words; and, moreover, felt herself, as it were, distinctly taken into confidence by the implied reference to the unhappy past, — old Nan melted.

"There, there, honey: don't ye take on so. We're jest powerful glad to get you here, we be. I was a tellin' Miss Hetty yesterday she couldn't live here alone, noways: we couldn't any of us stand it. Come along into the dinin'-room, an' Cæsar he'll give you a glass of his blackberry wine. Cæsar won't let anybody but hisself touch the blackberry wine, an' hain't this twenty year."

"Here, Cæsar! you, Cæsar! where be yer? Come right in here, you loafin' niggah." This was Nan's most affectionate nickname for her husband; it was always accompanied with a glance of proud admiration, which was the key to the seemingly opprobrious epithet, and revealed that all it really meant was a complacent satisfaction in her breast that her husband was in a position to loaf if he liked to, — a gentleman of leisure and dignity, so to speak, subject to no orders but her own.

Cæsar could hardly believe his ears when he heard himself called upon to bring a glass of his blackberry wine to Mrs. Sarah Little. This was not at all in keeping with the line of conduct which Nan had announced beforehand that she should pursue in regard to that lady. Bewildered by his perplexed meditations on this change of policy, he moved even more slowly than was his wont, and was presently still more bewildered by finding the glass snatched suddenly from his hand, with a sharp reprimand from Nan.

"You're asleep, ain't you? p'raps you'd better go back to bed, seein' it's nigh noon." "There, honey, you jest drink this, an' it 'll do you good," came in the next second from the same lips, in such dulcet tones, that Cæsar rubbed his head in sheer astonishment, and gazed with open mouth and eyes upon Nan, who was holding the glass to Sally's mouth, as caressingly as she would to a sick child's.

The battle was won; won by a tone and a tear; won, as, ever since the days of Goliath, so many battles have been won by the feebleness of weapons, and not by their might.

When two days later, James Little, more than half unwillingly, spite of his gratitude to Hetty, came to take his position as overseer at "Gunn's," he was met at the great gate by his wife, who had been watching there for him for an hour. He looked at her with undisguised wonder. There was a light in her eyes, a color in her cheeks, he had not seen there for many years. "Why, Sally!" he exclaimed, but gave no other expression to his amazement. She understood.

"Oh, Jim!" she said, "it is like heaven here: they're all so kind. I told you things would come round all right if we waited."

The new overseer found himself welcomed because he was Sally's husband, and the strangeness of this was a bewilderment indeed. He could hardly understand the atmosphere of cordial good feeling which seemed in so short time to have grown up between his wife and all the household. He had become so used to Sally's sweet sad face, that he did not know how great a charm it held for others; and he had never seen in her the manner which she now wore to every one. One day's kindly treatment had been to her like one day's sunlight to a drooping plant.

Hetty was relieved and glad. All her misgivings had vanished; and she found growing up in her heart a great tenderness toward Sally. She recollected well the bright rosy face Sally had worn only a few years before, and the contrast between it and her pale sorrow-stricken countenance now smote Hetty whenever she looked at her. Her sympathy, however, took no shape in words or caresses. She was too wise for that. She simply made it plain that Sally's place in the family was to be a fixed and a busy one.

"I shall look after the out-door things, Sally," she said. "I have done that ever since father was so poorly, and I like it best. I shall trust to you to keep the house going all straight. Old Nan is'nt much of a housekeeper, though she's a good cook: she needs looking after."

And so the new household entered on its first

summer. The crops sprang up, abundant and green: all the cattle throve and increased: the big garden bloomed full of its old-fashioned flowers; its wide borders of balm and lavender made the whole road-side sweet: the doors stood open, and the cheery sounds of brisk farm life were to be heard all day long. To all passers-by "Gunn's" seemed unchanged, unless it were that it had grown even more prosperous and active. But in the hall, two knobbed old canes which used to stand in the corner were hung by purple ribbons from the great antlers on the wall, and would never be taken down again. Hetty had hung them there the day after the funeral, and had laid the squire's riding-whip across them, saying to herself as she did so, —

"There! I'll keep those up there as long as I live, and I wonder what will become of them then or of the farm either," and she had a long and sad reverie, standing with the riding-whip in her hand in the doorway, and tying and untying the purple ribbons. But she shook the thought off at last, saying to herself, —

"Well, well, I don't suppose the farm 'll go begging. There are plenty of people that would be glad enough to have me give it to them. I expect it will have to go to Cousin Josiah after all;

but father couldn't abide him. It's a great pity I wasn't a boy, then I could have married and had children to take it." A sudden flush covered Hetty's face as she said this, and with a shamefaced, impatient twist of her expressive features, she ran in hastily and laid the whip above the canes.

The only thing which broke in on the even tenor of this summer at Gunn's was Cæsar's experiencing religion in a great revival at the Methodist church. Cæsar had been under conviction again and again; but, as old Nan said pathetically to her minister, there didn't seem to be "nothin' to ketch hold by in Cæsar." By the time his emotions had worked up to the proper climax for a successful result, he was "done tired out," and would "jest give right up" and "let go," and "there he was as bad's ever, if not wuss." Poor old Nan was a very ardent and sincere Christian, spite of her infirmities of temper, and she would wrestle in prayer with and for her husband till her black cheeks shone under streams of tears. She wrestled all the harder because the ungodly Cæsar would sometimes turn upon her, and in the most sarcastic and ungenerous way ask if he didn't keep his temper better "without religion than she did with it;"

upon which Nan would groan and travail in spirit, and beseech the Lord not to "go an' let her be a stumbler-block in Cæsar's way." The Squire's death had produced a great impression on Cæsar: from that day he had been, Nan declared, "quite a changed pusson;" and the impression deepened until three months later, in the course of a great midnight meeting in the Methodist church, Cæsar Gunn suddenly announced that he had "got religion." The one habit which it was hardest for Cæsar to give up, in his new character, was the habit of swearing. Profanity had never been strongly discountenanced at "Gunn's." The old Squire and the young Squire had both been in the habit of swearing, on occasion, as roundly as troopers! and black Cæsar was not going to be behind his masters, not he. So he, too, in spite of old Nan's protestations and entreaties, had become a confirmed swearer. It had really grown into so fixed a habit that the words meant nothing: it was no more than a trick of physical contortion of which a man may be utterly unconscious. How to break himself of this was Cæsar's difficulty.

"Yer see, Nan!" he said, "I dunno when it's a comin': the fust I know, it's said and done, an' what am I goin' to do 'bout it then, 'll yer tell me?" At last, Cæsar hit on a compromise which seemed to him a singularly happy one. To avoid saying "damn" was manifestly impossible: the word slipped out perpetually without giving him warning; as soon as he heard it, however, his righteous soul remorsefully followed up the syllable by, —

"Bress the Lord," in Stentorian tones. The compound ejaculation thus formed was one which nobody's gravity could resist; and the surprised and grieved expression with which poor Cæsar would look round upon an audience which he had thus convulsed was even more irresistible than the original expression. Everybody who came to "Gunn's" went away and said, —

"Have you heard the new oath Cæsar Gunn swears with since he got religion?" and "Damn bress the Lord" soon became a very by-word in the town.

IV.

EARLY in the autumn, Deacon Little's wife came one morning to the house and asked to see Hetty alone. Hetty met her with great coolness and remained standing, with evident purpose to regard the interview as simply one of business. As heartily as it was in Hetty Gunn's nature to dislike any one, and that was very heartily, she disliked Mrs. Little. Again and again, during the six months that James and Sally had been living in her house, Hetty had asked Deacon and Mrs. Little to come and spend the day with them there. The deacon always had come alone, bringing feeble apologies for Mrs. Little, on score of headaches, previous engagements, and so on; but privately, to Hetty, he had confessed the truth, saying,—

"You see, Hetty, she hasn't spoken to Sally yet; and she says she never will: just to see her on the street, gives her a dreadful nervous headache, sometimes for two days. Mrs. Little's nerves are too much for her always : she ain't strong, you know, Hetty."

"Nonsense!" exclaimed Hetty at last, bluntly. "It isn't nerves, it's temper, and a most unchristian temper too, begging your pardon. Deacon, I know she's your wife. If I were Jim, I'd never go near her, never, so long as she wouldn't speak to Sally. I shan't ask her again, and you may tell her so; and you may tell her, too, that I say I'd rather take my chance of being forgiven for what Sally's done than for what she's doing." And Hetty strode up and down her piazza wrathfully.

"There are plenty of people in town who do come here, and do speak to Sally," she continued; "and ever so many of them have told me how much they were coming to like her. She hasn't got any great force I know. If she had had, such a fellow as your Jim couldn't have led her away as he did: but she's got all the force the Lord gave her; and if ever there was a girl that repented for a sin, and atoned for it too, it's Sally; and I'd a good deal rather be in her place to-day, than in the place of any of the people that set themselves up as too good to speak to her. She's a loving, patient-souled creature, and she's been a real comfort to me ever since she came into my house; and anybody that won't speak to her needn't speak to me, that's all." Poor Deacon Little twirled his hat in his hands, and moved about uneasily on his chair, during Hetty's excited speech. When he spoke, his distress was so evident in his voice that. Hetty relented and was ashamed of herself instantly.

"Don't be too hard on Mrs. Little, Hetty," he said, "you know Jim was her favorite of all the children; and she can't never see it anyways but that Sally's been his ruin. Now I don't see it that way; and I've always tried to be good to Sally, in all ways that I could be, things being as they were at home. You know a man ain't always free to do's he likes, Hetty. He can't go against his wife, leastways not when she's feeble like Mrs. Little."

"No, no, Deacon Little," Hetty hastened to say, "I never meant to reproach you. Sally always says you've been good to her. I'm very sorry that I spoke so about Mrs. Little; not that I can take a word of it back, though," added Hetty, her anger still rising hotly at mention of the name; "but I'll never say a word to you about it again. It isn't fair."

Deacon Little repeated this conversation to his wife, and told Hetty that he had done so. It was therefore with great surprise that Hetty found herself on this morning face to face in her own home with Mrs. Little.

"What in the world can have brought her here?" thought Hetty, as she walked slowly towards the sitting-room, "no good I'll be bound;" and it was with a look almost of defiance that she stood before her, waiting for her to speak. Mrs. Little with all her immovability of prejudice was a timid woman, and moreover was especially afraid of Hetty Gunn. Hetty's independent, downright, out-spoken ways were alarming to her nervous, conservative, narrow-minded soul.

"I expect you're surprised to see me here, Hetty," she began.

"Very much," interrupted Hetty curtly, in a hard tone. A long silence ensued, which Hetty made no movement to break, but stood with her arms folded, looking Mrs. Little in the eye.

"I came — to — tell — to let you know — Mr. Little he wanted me to come and tell you — he didn't like to — " she stammered.

Hetty's quick instinct took alarm.

"If it's any thing you've got to say against that poor girl out there," pointing to the garden, where Sally was busy tying up chrysanthemums "you may as well save yourself the trouble. I shan't hear it," and Hetty looked her unwelcome visitor still more defiantly in the face. Mrs. Little colored, and stung at last into a command of her organs of speech, said, not without dignity:

"You needn't suppose that I wish to do any thing to injure the woman my son has married. It was Jim who asked his father to tell you—"

"For goodness' sake, do say what it is you've got to say, can't you?" burst out Hetty, impatiently. But Mrs. Little was not to be hurried. Between her uneasiness at being face to face with Hetty, and her false sense of embarrassment in speaking of the subject she had come to speak of, it took her a long time to make Hetty understand that poor Sally, finding that she was to be a mother again, had been afraid to tell Hetty herself, and had taken this method of letting her know the fact.

Hetty listened breathlessly, her blue eyes opening wide, and her cheeks growing red. She did not speak. Mrs. Little misinterpreted her silence.

"If you didn't want the baby here, I'd take it," she said almost beseechingly, "if Sally'd let me: it would break Jim's heart if they should have to leave here."

"Not want the baby!" shouted Hetty, in a voice which reached Sally in the garden, and made her look up, thinking she was called. "I should think you must be crazy, Mrs. Little;" and, with the involuntary words, there entered for the first time into her mind a wonder whether Mrs. Little's whole treatment of her son and his wife were not so monstrous as to warrant a doubt as to her sanity. "Not want the baby! Why I'd give half the farm to have a baby running about here. How could Sally help knowing I'd be glad?" and Hetty moved swiftly towards the door, to go and seek Sally. Recollecting herself suddenly, she turned, and, halting on the threshold, said in her hardest tone:

"Is there any thing else you wish to say?" There was ignominious dismissal in her tone, her look, her attitude; and Mrs. Little said hastily:

"Oh, no, nothing, nothing! I only want to tell you that I'd like to thank you, though, for all your kindness to Jim;" and Mrs. Little's lips quivered, and the tears came into her eyes. Hetty was unmoved by them.

"I think more of Sally than I do of Jim," she said severely. "It's all owing to Sally that he's got a chance to hold up his head again. Good morning, Mrs. Little;" and Hetty walked out of one door, leaving her guest to make her own way out of the other.

Sally found it hard to believe in Hetty's readiness to welcome her baby.

"Oh! you don't know, Hetty, how it will set everybody to talking again," said the poor girl. "You are so different from other folks. You can't understand. I don't suppose my children ever would be allowed to play with other children, do you?" she asked mournfully. "That was one thing which comforted me when my baby died. I thought she wouldn't live to have anybody despise her because she had had me for a mother. Somehow it don't seem fair, does it, Hetty, to have people punished for what their parents do? But the minister over at the Corners, that used to come and see me, he said that was what it meant in the Bible, where it said: 'Unto the third and fourth generation.' But I can't think it's so bad as that. You don't believe, Hetty, do you, that if I should have several children, and they should be married, that their grandchildren would ever hear any thing about me, how wicked I had been: do you, Hetty?"

"No, indeed, child!" said Hetty sharply, feeling as if she should cry. "Of course I don't believe any such thing; and, if I did, I wouldn't worry over it. Why, I don't even know my great-grandmother's name," she laughed, "much less whether she were good or bad."

"Oh, but the bad things last so!" said Sally. "Nobody says any thing about the good things: it's always the bad ones. I don't see why people like to: if they didn't, there'd be some chance of a thing's being forgotten."

"Never you mind, Sally," said Hetty, in a tone unusually caressing for her. "Never you mind, nobody talks about you now, except to say the good things; and you are always going to stay with me as long as I live, and when that baby comes we'll just wonder how we ever got along without him."

"Oh, Hetty, you're just one of the Lord's angels!" cried Sally.

"Humph!" said Hetty. "I hope he's got better ones. There wasn't much angel about me this morning when that mother-in-law of yours was here, I can tell you. I wonder if she'll have the heart to keep away after the baby's born."

"I thought of that, too," said Sally, timidly.

"If it should be a boy, I think maybe she'd be pleased. She always did worship Jim. That's the reason she hates me so," sighed Sally.

It was the last of March before the longed-for baby came. Never did baby have a better welcome. It was as if three mothers had awaited his coming. Hetty's happiness was far greater than Sally's, and Nan's was hardly less. Hetty had been astonished at herself for the passionate yearning she had felt towards the little unborn creature from the beginning, and, when she took the little fellow in her arms, her first thought was, "Dear me! if mothers feel any more than I feel now, how can they bear it?" Turning to Jim, she exclaimed, "Oh, Jim! I'm sure you ought to be happy now. We'll name this little chap after you, James Little, Junior."

"No!" said Jim, doggedly, "I'll not hand down that name. The sooner it is forgotten the better." All the sunshine and peace of his new home had not been enough wholly to brighten or heal Jim's wounded spirit. Hetty had found herself baffled at every turn by a sort of inertia of sadness, harder to deal with than any other form of mental depression.

"You're very wrong, Jim," replied Hetty,

earnestly. "The name is your own to make or to mar, and you ought to be proud to hand it down."

"You can't judge about that, Hetty," said Jim. "It stands to reason that you can't have any idea about the feeling of being disgraced. I don't believe a man can ever shake it off in this world: if he can in any other, I have my doubts. I don't know what the orthodox people ever wanted to get up their theory of a hell for. A man can be a worse hell to himself, than any hell they can invent to put him into. I know that."

"Jim!" exclaimed Hetty, "how dare you speak so, with this dear little innocent baby's eyes looking up at you?"

"That's just the reason," answered Jim, bitterly. "If this baby hadn't come, there seemed to be some chance of our outgrowing the memory of the things we'd like to forget and have forgotten. But this just rakes it all up again as bad as ever. You'll see: you don't know people so well as Sally and I do."

Before many weeks had passed, Hetty was forced to admit that Jim was partly in the right. Neighbor after neighbor, under the guise of a friendly interest in the baby, took occasion to go over all the details of the first baby's life and death; and there was, in their manner to Sally, a certain new and pitying condescension which filled Hetty with wrath.

"What a mercy 'tis, 'tis a boy," said one visitor sanctimoniously to Hetty, as they left Sally's room together. Hetty turned upon her like lightning.

"I'd like to know what you mean by that," she said sharply. The woman hesitated, and at last said:

"Why you know, of course, such things are not so much consequence to men."

"Such things as what?" said Hetty, bluntly. "I don't understand you." When at last her visitor put her meaning into unmistakable words, Hetty wheeled (they were walking down the long pine-shaded avenue together); stood still; and folding her arms on her bosom said:

"There! that was what I wanted. I thought if you were driven to putting it into plain English, perhaps you'd see how abominable it was to think it."

"No, no, you needn't try to smooth it down," she continued, interrupting her guest's efforts to mollify her by a few deprecating words. "You can't unsay it, now it's said; and saying it's no worse than thinking it. I don't envy you your thoughts, though. I've always stood up for Sally, and I always shall, and anybody that is stupid enough to suppose, because I stand up for her, I justify what she did that was wrong, is welcome: I don't care. Sally is a good, patient, loving woman to-day; I don't know anybody more so: I, for one, respect her. I wish I could be half as patient;" and Hetty stooped, and, picking up a handful of the pine-needles with which the road was thickly strewn, crumbled them up fiercely in her hands, and tossing the dust high in the air, exclaimed:

"I wouldn't give that for the character of any woman that can't believe in another woman's having thoroughly repented of having done wrong."

"Oh! nobody doubts that Sally has repented," said the embarrassed visitor.

"Oh, they don't?" said Hetty, in a sarcastic tone; "well then I'd like to ask them what they mean by treating her as they do. I'd like to ask them what the Lord does to sinners that repent. He says they are to come and be with him in Heaven, I believe; and I'd like to know whether after He's taken them to Heaven, they're going to be reminded every minute of all the sins they've repented of. Oh, but I've no patience with it!"

As Hetty was walking slowly back to the house after this injudicious outburst, she met Dr. Eben Williams coming down the avenue. Her first impulse was to plunge into the shrubbery, on the right hand or the left, and escape him. The baby was now four weeks old, and yet Hetty had never till to-day seen the doctor. It had been a very sore point between her and Sally, that Sally would persist in having this young Dr. Williams from the "Corners," instead of old Dr. Tuthill, who had been the family doctor at "Gunn's" for nearly fifty years. It was the only quarrel that Hetty and Sally had ever had; and it came near being a very serious one: but Hetty suddenly recollected herself, and exclaiming:

"Why bless me, Sally, I haven't any right to decide what doctor you're to have when you're sick; I'll never say another word about it; only you needn't expect me ever to speak to that Eben Williams; I never expected to see him under my roof," she dropped the subject and never alluded to it again.

Her first impulse, as we said, when she saw the obnoxious doctor coming towards her now, was to fly; her second one of anger with herself for the first.

"I'm on my own ground," she thought with some of the old Squire's honest pride stirring her veins, "I think I will not run away from the popinjay."

It was hard to know just how such a dislike to Dr. Eben Williams had grown up in Hetty's friendly heart. He had come some four years before to practise medicine at Lonway Four Corners. His bright and cordial face, his social manner, his superior education, readiness, and resource, had quickly won away many patients from old Dr. Tuthill, who still drove about the country as he had driven for half a century, with a ponderous black leather case full of calomel and jalap swung under his sulky. A few old families, the Gunns among the number, adhered faithfully to the old doctor, and became bitter partisans against the new one.

"Let him stick to the Corners: if they like him there, they're welcome to him. He needn't be trying to get all Welbury besides," they said angrily. "Welbury's done very well for a doctor, these good many years: since before Eben Williams was born, for that matter;" and words ran high in the warfare. Squire Gunn was one of the most violent of Dr. Williams's opposers; and when, a few days before his death, old Dr. Tuthill had timidly suggested that it might be well to have a consultation, the Squire broke out with:

"Not that damned Eben Williams then. I won't have that damned rascal set foot in this house. You're a fool, Tuthill, to let that young upstart get all your practice as he's a doing."

The old man smiled sadly. He did not in the least share his friends' hostility to the handsome, young, and energetic physician who was so plainly soon to be his successor in the county.

"Ah, Squire!" he said, "you forget how old you and I are. It is nearly my time to pass on, and make room for a younger man. Eben's a good doctor. I'd rather he'd have the circuit here than anybody I know."

"Damned interloper! let him wait till you're dead," growled the Squire. "He shan't have a hand in finishing me off at any rate. I don't want any of their new-fangled notions." And the Squire died as he had lived, on the old plan, with the old doctor.

When Eben Williams saw that he was about to meet Hetty Gunn, his emotions were hardly less conflicting than hers. He, too, would have liked to escape the meeting, for he had understood clearly that his presence in her house was most unwelcome to her. But he, too, had his own pride, as distinct and as strong as hers, and at the very moment that Hetty was saying to herself, "I'm on my own ground: I won't run away from the popinjay," Dr. Eben was thinking in his heart, "What a fool I am to care a straw about meeting her! I'm about my own business, and she is an obstinate simpleton."

The expressions of their faces as they met, and passed, with cold bows, were truly comical; each so thoroughly conscious of the other's antagonism, and endeavoring to look unconscious of it.

"By Jove, she's got a charming face, if she didn't look so obstinate," said Dr. Eben to himself, as he hurried on.

"He looked at me as he'd have looked at a snake," thought Hetty. "I guess he's an honest fellow after all. He's got a handsome beard of his own."

When she entered Sally's room, Sally exclaimed, "Oh, Hetty! didn't you meet the doctor?"

"Yes," said Hetty, coolly. Sally looked wistfully at her for a few seconds. "Oh, Hetty!" she said, "I thought, perhaps, if you saw him, you'd like him better."

"I never said any thing against his looks, did I?" laughed Hetty. "He is a very handsome man: he is the handsomest man I ever saw, if that's all!"

"But it isn't all; it isn't any thing!" exclaimed Sally. "If he were an ugly dwarf, I should love him just as well. Oh, Hetty, if you only knew how good he was to me, when I was sick seven years ago! I should have died if it hadn't been for him. There wasn't a woman at the Corners that ever came near me, except Mrs. Patrick, the Irish woman I boarded with; and, he used to stop and make broth for me, on my stove, with his own hands, and sit and hold the baby on his knees, and talk to me so beautifully about her. He just kept me alive."

Hetty's face flushed. Sally had never told her so much before; she could not help a glow at her heart, at the picture of the handsome young doctor sitting with the poor, outcast baby on his knees, and comforting the poor outcast mother. But Hetty was a Gunn; and, as Dr. Eben had said, obstinate. She could not forget her partisanship for Dr. Tuthill. She was even all the angrier with the young doctor for being so clever, so kind, so skilful, so handsome, and so pleasant, that everybody wanted him.

"I dare say," she replied. "He'd do any thing to curry favor. He's been determined from the first to get all the practice of the whole county, and I suppose as soon as Doctor Tuthill dies, he'll have it; and he may as well, for I don't doubt he's a good doctor: but I think it was a mean underhand thing to come in here and try to cut another man out."

"Why, Hetty!" remonstrated Sally, in a tone of unusual vehemence for her. "Why, Hetty; there wasn't any doctor at the Corners: he didn't cut anybody out there; and I'm sure they needed a doctor bad enough; and it was his native place too."

"Oh! that's all very well to say," answered Hetty. "It's a likely story, isn't it, that anybody'd settle in Lonway Four Corners, just for the little practice there is in that handful of a village. He knew very well he'd get Welbury, and Springton, and all the county."

"But, Hetty," persisted Sally. "He wasn't to blame, if people in these towns sent for him, hearing how good he was. Indeed, indeed, Hetty, he don't care for the money. He wouldn't take a cent from Jim, and he never does from poor people. I've heard him say a dozen times, that he should have come home to live on the old farm, even if they hadn't needed a doctor there: he loves the country so, he can't be happy in the city; and he loves every stick and stone of the old farm."

"Humph!" said Hetty. "He looks like a country fellow, doesn't he, with his fine clothes, and his gauntlet gloves! Don't tell me! I say he is a popinjay, with all his learning. Now don't talk any more about it, little woman, for your cheeks are getting too red," and Hetty took up the baby, and began to toss him and talk to him.

Hetty knew in her heart that she was unjust. More than she would have owned to herself, and still more than she would have acknowledged to Sally, she had admired Eben Williams's honest, straightforward, warm-hearted face. But she preferred to dislike Eben Williams: her father had disliked him, and had said he should never set foot in the house; and Hetty felt a certain sort of filial obligation to keep up the animosity.

But Nature had other plans for Hetty. In fact if one were disposed to be superstitious, one might well have said that fate itself had determined to thwart Hetty's resolution of hostility.

V.

SALLY did not recover rapidly from her illness: her long mental suffering had told upon her vitality, and left her unprepared for any strain. The little baby also languished, sharing its mother's depressed condition. Day after day, Doctor Eben came to the house. His quick step sounded in the hall and on the stairs; his voice rang cheery, whenever the door of Sally's room stood open. Hetty found herself more and more conscious of his presence: each day she felt a half guilty desire to see him again; she caught herself watching for his knock, listening for his step; she even went so far as to wonder in a half impatient way why he never sent for her, to give her the directions about Sally, instead of giving them to the nurse. She little dreamed that Doctor Eben was as anxious to avoid seeing her, as she had been to avoid seeing him. He had a strangely resentful feeling towards Hetty, as if she were a personal friend who had been treacherous to him. She was the only one of all the partisans of Doctor Tuthill that he could not sympathize with and heartily forgive. He would have found it very hard to explain why he thus singled out Hetty, but he had done so from the outset. Strange forerunning instinct of love, which uttered its prophecy in an unknown tongue in an alien country! There came a day before long, when Doctor Eben and Hetty were forced to forget all their prejudices, and to come together on a common ground, where no antagonisms could exist.

Sally and the baby were both very ill. Hetty, in her inexperience of illness, had not realized how serious a symptom Sally's long continued prostration was. In her own busy and active life, the days flew by almost uncounted: she was out early and late, walking or riding over the farm; and when she came back to Sally's room, and found her always with the same placid smile, and fair untroubled face, and heard always the same patient reply, "Very comfortable, thank you, dear Hetty," it never occurred to her that any thing was wrong. It seemed strange to her that the baby was so still, that he neither cried nor laughed like other babies; and it seemed to her very hard for

Sally to have to be shut up in the house so long: but this was all; she was totally unprepared for any thought of danger, and the shock was terrible to her, when the thought came. It was on a sunny day in May, one of those incredible summer days which New England sometimes flashes out like frost-set jewels in her icy spring. Hetty had listened, as usual, to hear the Doctor leave Sally's room: she was more than usually impatient to have him go, for she was waiting to take in to Sally a big basket of arbutus blossoms which old Cæsar had gathered, and had brought to Hetty with a characteristic speech.

"Seems's if the Lord meant 'em for baby's cheeks, don't it, Miss Hetty? they're so rosy."

"Our poor little man's cheeks are not so pink yet," said Hetty, and as she looked at the pearly pink bells nestling in their green leaves, she sighed, and wished that the baby did not look so pale. "But he'll be all right as soon as we can get him out of doors in the June sunshine," she added, and turned from the dining-room into the hall, with the great basket of arbutus in her hand. As she turned, she gave a cry, and dropped her flowers: there sat Dr. Eben, in a big arm-chair, by the doorway. He sprang to pick up the flowers. Hetty looked at him without speaking. "I was waiting here to see you, Miss Gunn," he said, as he gave back the flowers. "I am very sorry to be obliged to speak to you," — here Hetty's eyes twinkled, and a slight, almost imperceptible, but very comic grimace passed over her face. She was thinking to herself, "Honest, that! I expect he is very sorry," — "I am very sorry to have to speak to you about Mrs. Little," he continued; "but I think it is my duty to tell you that she is sinking very fast."

"What! Sally! what is the matter with her?" exclaimed Hetty. "Come right in here, doctor;" and she threw open the sitting-room door, and, leading him in, sank into the nearest chair, and said, like a little child:

"Oh, dear! what shall I do?"

Dr. Eben looked at her for a second, scrutinizingly.

This was not the sort of person he had expected to see in Miss Hetty Gunn. This was an impulsive, outspoken, loving woman, without a trace of any thing masculine about her, unless it were a certain something in the quality of her frankness, which was masculine rather than feminine; it was more purely objective than women's frankness is wont to be: this Dr. Eben thought out later; at present, he only thought:

"Poor girl! I've got to hurt her sadly."

"You don't mean that Sally's going to die, do you?" said Hetty, in a clear, unflinching tone.

"I am afraid she will, Miss Gunn," replied Dr. Eben, "not immediately; perhaps not for some months: but there seems to be a general failure of all the vital forces. I cannot rouse her, body or soul."

"Nonsense!" said Hetty. "If rousing is all she wants, surely we can rouse her somehow. Isn't there any thing wrong with her anywhere?"

Dr. Eben smiled in spite of himself at this offhand, non-professional view of the case; but he answered, sadly:

"Not what you mean by any thing wrong; if there were, it would be easier to cure her."

Hetty knitted her brows, and looked at him in her turn, scrutinizingly. "Have you had patients like her before?"

"Yes," said Dr. Eben.

"Did they all die? Didn't you cure one?" continued Hetty, inexorably.

"I have known persons in such a condition to recover," said Dr. Eben, with dignity; "but not by the help of medicine so much as by an entire change of conditions."

"What do you mean by conditions?" said

Hetty, never having heard, in her simple and healthful life, of anybody's needing what is called a "change of scene." Dr. Eben smiled again, and, as he smiled, he noted with an involuntary professional delight the clear, fine skin, the firm flesh, the lustrous eye, the steady poise of every muscle in this woman, who was catechising him, with so evident a doubt as to his skill and information.

"I hardly think, Miss Gunn," he went on, "that I could make you understand, in your superb health, just all I mean by change of conditions. It means change of food, air, surroundings; every thing in short, which addresses itself to the senses. It means an entire new set of nerve impressions."

"Sally isn't in the least nervous," broke in Hetty. "She's always as quiet as a mouse."

"You mean that she isn't in the least fidgety," replied the doctor. "That is quite another thing. Some of the most nervous people I know have absolute quiet of manner. Mrs. Little's nervous system has been for several years under a terrible strain. When I was first called to her, I thought her trouble and suffering would kill her; and I didn't think it would take so long. But it is that which is killing her now."

Hetty was not listening: she was thinking very perplexedly of what the doctor had said a few moments before; interrupting him now, she said, "Would it do Sally good to take her to another place? that is easily done." Dr. Ebèn hesitated.

"I think sea-air might help her; but I am not sure," he replied.

"Would you go with us?" asked Hetty. "She wouldn't go without you." The doctor hesitated again. He looked into Hetty's eyes: they were fixed on his as steadily, as unembarrassedly, as if he and Hetty had been comrades for years. "What a woman she is," he thought to himself, "to coolly ask me to become their travelling physician, when for six weeks I have been coming to the house every day, and she would not even speak to me!"

"I am not sure that I could, Miss Gunn," he replied. Hetty's face changed. A look of distress stamped every feature.

"Oh, Dr. Williams, do!" she exclaimed. "Sally would never go without you; and she will die, you say, unless she has change." Then hesitating, and turning very red, Hetty stammered, "I can pay you any thing — which would be necessary to compensate you: we have money enough." Dr. Eben bowed, and answered with some asperity:

"The patients that I had hesitancy about leaving are patients who pay me nothing. It is not in the least a question of money, Miss Gunn."

"Forgive me," exclaimed Hetty, "I did not know — I thought —"

"Your thought was a perfectly natural one, Miss Gunn," interrupted the doctor, pitying her confusion. "I have never had need to make my profession a source of income: I have no ambition to be rich; and, as I am alone in the world, I can afford to do what many other physicians could not."

"When can you tell if you could go?" continued Hetty, not apparently hearing what the doctor had said.

"She only thinks of me as she would of a chair or a carriage which would make her friend more comfortable," thought the doctor; "and why should she think of me in any other way," he added, impatient with himself for the selfish thought.

"To-morrow," said he, curtly. "If I can go, I will; and there is no time to be lost."

Hetty nodded her head, but did not speak another word: she was too near crying; and to have cried in the presence of Dr. Eben Williams would have mortified Hetty to the core.

"Oh, to think," she said to herself, "that, after all, I should have to be under such obligations to that man! But it is all for Sally's sake, poor dear child. How good he is to her! If he were anybody else, I should like him with all my heart."

The next morning, as Dr. Williams walked slowly up the avenue, he saw Hetty standing in the doorway, shading her eyes with her hand and looking towards him. The morning sun shone full upon her, and made glints of golden light here and there in her thick brown curls. Hetty had worn her hair in the same style for fifteen years; short, clustering curls close to her head on either side, and a great mass of curls falling over a comb at the back. If Hetty had a vanity it was of her hair; and it was a vanity one was forced to forgive, — it had such excellent reason for being. The picture which she made in the doorway, at this moment, Dr. Eben never forgot: a strange pleasure thrilled through him at the sight. As he drew near, she ran down the steps towards him; ran down with no more thought or consciousness of the appearance of welcoming him, than if she had been a child of seven: she was impatient to know whether Sally could go to the sea-shore. This man who approached held the decision in his hands; and he was, at that moment, no more to Hetty than any messenger bringing word which she was eager to hear. But Dr. Eben would have been more or less than man, could he have seen, unmoved, the swift motion, the outstretched hands, the eager eyes, the bright cheeks, the sunlit hair, of the beautiful woman who ran to meet him.

"Well?" was all that Hetty said, as, panting for want of breath, she turned as shortly as a wild creature turns, and began to walk by Dr. Eben's side. He forgot, for the instant, all the old antagonisms; he forgot that, until yesterday, he had never spoken with Hetty Gunn; and, meeting her eager gaze with one about as eager, he said in a familiar tone:

"Yes; well! I am going."

Hetty stopped short, and, looking up at him, exclaimed:

"Oh, I am so glad!"

The words were simple enough, but the tone made them electric. The doctor felt the blood mounting in his face, under the unconscious look of this middle-aged child. She did not perceive his expression. She did not perceive any thing, except the fact that Sally's doctor would help her take Sally away, and save Sally's life. She continued:

"We'll take her to 'The Runs.' Did you ever go there, doctor? It is only a day's journey from here, the loveliest little sea-side place I ever saw. It isn't like the big sea-side places with their naked rocks, and their great, cruel, thundering beaches. I hate those. They make me sad and desperate. I know Sally wouldn't like them. But this little place is as sweet and quiet as a lake; and yet it is the sea. It is hugged in between two tongues of land, and there are ever so many little threads of the sea, running way up into the meadows, which are thick with high strong grass, so different from all the grasses we have here. I buy salt hay from there every year, and the cattle like it, just a little of it, as well as we like a bit of broiled bacon for breakfast. There is a nice bit of beach, too, — real beach; but there are trees on it, and it looks friendly: not as if it were just made on purpose for wrecks to drift up on, like the big beaches: oh, but I hate a great, long sea-beach! There is a farm-house there, not two minutes' walk from this beach, where they always take summer boarders. In July it wouldn't be pleasant, because it is crowded;

but now it will be empty, and we can have it all to ourselves. There is a dear, old, retired, sea captain there, too, who takes people out in such a nice sail-boat. I shall keep Sally and the baby out on the water all day long. I am afraid you will find it very dull, Dr. Williams. Do you like the sea? Of course you will stay with us all the time. I don't mean in the least, that you are to come only once a day to see Sally, as you do here. You will be our guest, you understand. I dare say you will do more to cure Sally than all the sea-air and all the medicine put together. She has had so few people to love in this world, poor girl, that those she does love are very dear to her. She is more grateful to you than to anybody else in the world."

"Except you, Miss Gunn," replied the doctor, earnestly. "You have done for her far more than I ever could. I could show only a personal sympathy; but you have added to the personal sympathy material aid."

"Yes, yes, I know," said Hetty, absently. She did not wish to hear any thing said about this. "We can set out to-morrow, if you can be ready," she continued. "I shall have Cæsar drive the horses over next week. They can't very well be spared this week. The worst thing is, we have to set out so early in the morning, and Sally is always so much weaker then. Could you"— Hetty hesitated, and fairly stammered in her embarrassment. "Couldn't you come over here to-night and sleep, so as to be here when she first wakes up? You might do something to help her." Before Hetty had finished her sentence, her face was crimson. Dr. Eben's was full of a humorous amusement. Already, in twenty-four hours, had it come to this, that Hetty was urging that popinjay Dr. Ebenezer Williams, to come and sleep under her roof? The twinkle in his face showed her plainly what he was thinking. He began to reply:

"You are very kind, Miss Gunn"— Hetty interrupted him:

"No, I am not at all kind, Dr. Williams; and I see you are laughing at me, because I've had to speak to you, after all, as if I liked you. But, of course, you understand that it is all for Sally's sake. If I were to be ill myself, I should have Dr. Tuthill," said Hetty, in a tone meant to be very resolute and dignified, but only succeeding in being comical.

The doctor bowed ceremoniously, replying:

"I will be as frank as you are, Miss Gunn. As

you say, 'of course' I understand that any apparent welcome which you extend to me is entirely for Mrs. Little's sake; and that it is sorely against your will that you have been obliged to speak to me; and that it is solely in my capacity as physician that I am asked to sleep under your roof to-night; and I beg your pardon for saying that I accept the invitation in that capacity, and no other, solely because I believe it will be for the interest of my patient that I do so. Good morning, Miss Gunn," and, as at that moment they reached the house, Dr. Eben bowed again as ceremoniously as before, sprang up the piazza steps, and ran up the staircase, two steps at a time, to Sally's room. Hetty stood still in the doorway: she felt herself discomfited. She was half angry, half amused. She did not like what the doctor had said; but she admitted to herself that it was precisely what she would have said in his place.

"I don't blame him," she thought, "I don't blame him a bit; but, it is horridly disagreeable. I don't see how we're ever to get on; and it is so provoking, for, if he were anybody else, we'd be real good friends. He isn't in the least what I thought he was. I hope he won't come over before tea. It would be awkward enough. But then, he's got to take all his meals with us at 'The Runs.' Oh, dear!" and Hetty went about her preparations for the journey, with feelings by no means of unalloyed pleasure.

No danger of Dr. Eben's coming before tea. It was very late when he appeared, valise in hand, and said in a formal tone to Hetty, who met him at the door, in fact had been nervously watching for him for four whole hours:

"I am very sorry to see you still up, Miss Gunn. I ought to have recollected to tell you that I should not be here until late: I have been saying good-by to my patients. Will you have the kindness to let me be shown to my room?" and like a very courteous traveller, awaiting a landlady's pleasure, he stood at foot of the stairs.

With some confusion of manner, and in a constrained tone, unlike her usual cheery voice, Hetty replied:

"The next door to Sally's, doctor." She wished to say something more, but she could not think of a word.

"What a fool I am!" she mentally ejaculated, as the doctor, with a hasty "good-night," entered his room. "What a fool I am to let him make me so uncomfortable. I don't see what it is. I wish I hadn't asked him to go."

"That woman's a jewel!" the doctor was saying to himself the other side of the door: "she is as honest as a man could be. I didn't know there could be any thing so honest in shape of a woman under fifty: she doesn't look a day over twenty-five; but, they say she's nearly forty; it's the strangest thing in life she's never married. I'll wager any thing, she's wishing this minute I was in Guinea; but she'll put it through bravely for sake of Sally, as she calls her, and I'll keep out of her way all I can. If it weren't for the confounded notion she's taken up against me, I'd like to know her. She's a woman a man could make a friend of, I do believe," and Dr. Eben jumped into bed, and was fast asleep in five minutes, and dreamed that Hetty came towards him, dressed like an Indian, with her brown curls stuck full of painted porcupine quills, and a tomahawk brandished in her hand.

VI.

THE journey was a hard one, though so short. How many times an hour did Hetty bless the good fortune which had given them Dr. Williams for an escort! Sally had been so much excited and pleased at the prospect of the trip to the sea-shore, that she had seemed in the outset far stronger than she really was. Before mid-day a reaction had set in, and she had grown so weak that the doctor was evidently alarmed. The baby disturbed, and frightened by the noise and jar, had wailed almost incessantly; and Hetty was more nearly at her wits' end than she had ever been in her life. It was piteous to see her, — usually so brisk, so authoritative, so unhesitating, — looking helplessly into the face of the doctor, and saying:

"Oh, what shall we do! what shall we do!" At last, the weary day came to an end; and when Hetty saw her two sufferers quietly asleep in snowy beds, in a great airy room, with a blazing log-fire on the hearth, she drew a long breath, and said to the doctor:

"This is the most awful day I ever lived through."

Dr. Eben smiled. "You have had a life singularly free from troubles, Miss Gunn."

"No!" said Hetty, "I've had a great deal. But there has always been something to do. The only things one can't bear, it seems to me, are where one can't do any thing, like to-day: that poor little baby crying, crying, and nothing to be done, but to wait for him to stop; and Sally looking as if she would die any minute; and that screaming steam-engine whirling us all along as if we were only dead freight. I suppose if Sally had died, we should have had to keep right on, shouldn't we?"

"Yes," said the doctor. Something in his tone arrested Hetty's ear. She looked at him inquiringly; then she said slowly:

"I understand you. I am ashamed. We were only three people out of hundreds: it is just like life, isn't it: how selfish we are without realizing it! It isn't of any consequence how or where or when any one of us dies: the train must keep right on. I see."

"Yes," said the doctor again: and this monosyllable meant even more than the other. Dr. Eben was a philosopher. Epictetus, and that most royal of royal emperors, Marcus Aurelius, had been his masters: their words were ever present with him. "It is not possible that the nature of the universe, either through want of power or want of skill, has made a mistake;" "nothing happens to any man which he is not formed by nature to bear,"—were hourly watchwords of thought with him. In this regard he and Hetty were alike, though they had reached their common standpoint by different roads: he by education and reasoning, and a profound admiration for the ancient classics; she by instinct and healthfulness of soul, and a profound love for that old Massachusetts militiaman, her grandfather.

"The Runs" was, as Hetty had said, one of the loveliest of sea-side places. Dr. Eben, who was familiar with all the well-known sea-side resorts in America, was forced to admit that this little nook had a charm of its own, unlike all the others. The epithet "hugged in," which Hetty had used, was the very phrase to best convey it. It was at the mouth of a small river, which, as it drew near the sea, widened so suddenly that it looked like a lake. The country, for miles about, was threaded by little streams of water: which of them were sea making up, and which were river coming down, it was hard to tell. In early morning they were blue as the sky overhead; at sunset they glowed like a fiery net, suddenly flung over the grasses and rushes. Great flocks of marsh birds dwelt year after year in these cool, green labyrinths, and made no small part of the changeful beauty of the picture, rising sometimes, suddenly, in a dusky cloud, and floating away, soaring, and sinking, and at last dropping out of sight again, as suddenly as they had risen. The meadows were vivid green in June, vivid claret in October: no other grass spreads such splendor of tint on so superb a palette, as the salt-marsh grasses on the low, wide stretches of some of New England's southern shores. Sailing down this river, and keeping close to the left-hand bank, one came almost unawares on a sharp bend to the left: here the river suddenly ended, and the sea began; the rushes and reeds and high grasses ceased; a low, rocky barrier stayed them. Rounding this point, lo, your boat swayed instantly to the left: a gentle surf-wave took possession of you, and irresistibly bore you towards a yellow sand beach, which curved inward like a reaper's sickle, not more than a quarter of a mile long, from the handle to the shining point; smooth and glistening, strewn with polished pebbles and tiny shells, it seemed some half-hidden magic beach on which shallops of fairies might any moment come to moor. On the farther point, so close to the sea that it seemed to rise out of the water, stood a high stone lighthouse, with a revolving light, whose rays swept the open sea for many miles. The opposite river bank was a much higher one, and ran farther out to sea. On this promontory was Safe Haven, a small, thickly settled town, whose spires and house-tops, as seen from the beach at "The Runs," looked always like a picture, painted on the sky; white on gray in the morning, gray on crimson at sunset. The farmhouse of which we have spoken stood only a few rods back from the beach, and yet it had green fields on either hand; and a row of Balm of Gilead trees in front; an old and sandy road, seldom disturbed by wheels, ran between these trees and the house, and rambled down towards the light-house. Wild pea and pimpernel made this road gay; white clover and wild rose made it fragrant; and there branched off from it a lane, on which if you turned and strayed back into the fields, a mile or so, you came to thickets of wild azalia, and tracts of pink laurel; and, a little way farther in, you came to fresh-water ponds which in July were white with lilies. No storm ever lashed the water high on the beach at "The Runs"; no sultriest summer calm ever stilled it; the even rhythm and delightsome cooling of its waves seemed to obey a law of their own, quite independent of the great booming sea outside the light-house bar.

In the quiet, and the beauty, and the keen salt air of this charmed spot, poor Sally Little lifted up her head, and began to live again, like a flower taken from desert sands and set by a spring. The baby also bloomed like a rose. In an incredibly short time, both mother and child had so altered that one would hardly have known them. The days went by, to them all, as days go by for children: unnamed, uncounted; only marked by joy of sleep, and the delight of waking. In after years, when Hetty looked back upon these weeks, they seemed to her, not like a dream, which is usually the heart's first choice of a phrase to describe the swift flight of a happy time, but like a few days spent on some other planet, where, for the interval, she had been changed into a sort of supernatural child. Except at night, they were never in the house. The harsh New England May laid aside for them all its treacheries, and was indeed the month of spring. Their mornings they spent on the water, rowing or sailing; their afternoons in driving through the budding and blossoming country. Always the baby lay in Hetty's lap: from the beginning, his nurse had found herself perpetually set aside by Hetty's imperious affection. As Eben Williams looked, day after day, on the picture which Hetty and the baby made, he found himself day after day more and more bewildered by Hetty. She had adopted towards him a uniform manner of cordial familiarity, which had in it, however, no shade of intimacy. If Hetty had been the veriest coquette living, she could not have devised a more effectual charm to a man of Eben Williams's temperament. He had come out unscathed from many sieges which had been laid to him by women. He knew very well the ordinary methods, the atmosphere of the average wooing or wooable woman, and he was proof against them all. He was thirty years old and he had never yet been in love. But this woman, who treated him with the same easy, unconscious frankness with which men treat men, who never seemed to observe his going or his coming, otherwise than as it might affect her friend's need of him as a physician; this woman who seemed all mother while she was holding the baby, and all boy while she was trying, under old Captain Mayhew's guidance to learn to sail a boat; this woman who was a spinster in years, and a child in simplicity and directness; who was beautiful, and never once thought of her beauty; who was alone, and never seemed lonely: she was a perpetual problem and fascination to him. Dr. Eben was not usually given to concerning himself much as to other people's opinion of him: but he found himself for ever wondering what Hetty Gunn thought of him; whether she were beginning to lose any of her old prejudice against him; and whether, after this seaside idyl were over, he should ever see her again. The more he pondered, the less he could solve the question. No wonder. The simple truth was that Hetty was not thinking about him at all. She had accepted the whole situation with frankness and good sense: she found him kind, helpful, cheery, and entertaining; the embarrassments she had feared, did not arise, and she was very glad of it. She often said to herself: "The doctor is very sensible. He does not show any foolish feeling of resentment;" and she felt a sincere and increasing gratitude to him, because Sally and her child were fast regaining health under his care. But, beyond this, Hetty did not occupy her thoughts with Dr. Eben. It had never been her way to think about men, as most women think about them: good comradeship seemed to be all that she was capable of towards a man. Dr. Eben said this to himself hundreds of times each day; and then hundreds of other times each day, as he watched the looks which she bent on the baby in her arms, he knew that he had said what was not true; that there must be unstirred depths in her nature, which only the great forces of love could move. All this time Dr. Eben fancied that he was simply analyzing Hetty as a psychological study. He would have admitted frankly to any one, that she interested him more than any woman he had ever seen, puzzled him more, occupied his thoughts more; but that he could be in love with this rather eccentric middle-aged woman, beautiful though she was, Dr. Eben would have warmly denied. His ideal maiden, the woman whom he had been for ten years confidently expecting some day to find, woo, and win, was quite unlike Hetty; unlike even what Hetty must have been in her youth: she was to be slender and graceful; gentle as a dove; vivacious, but in no wise opinionated, gracious and suave and versed in all elegancies; cultured too, and of a rare, fine wit: so easy is it for the heart to garnish its unfilled chambers, and picture forth the sort of guest it will choose to entertain. Meanwhile, by doors which the heart knows not of, quietly enters a guest of quite different presence, takes up abode, is lodged and fed by angels, till grown a very monarch in possession and control, it suddenly surprises the heart into an absolute and unconditional allegiance; and this is like what the apostle meant, when he said,—

"The kingdom of God cometh not by observation."

When Hetty said to Dr. Eben, one night, "I really think we must go home. Sally seems perfectly well, and baby too: do you not think it will be quite safe to take them back?" he gave an actual start, and colored. Professionally, Dr. Eben was more ashamed of himself in that instant than he had ever been in his life. He had absolutely forgotten, for many days, that it was in the capacity of a physician that he was living on this shore of the sea. They had been at "The Runs" now two months; and, except in his weekly visits to Lonway Corners, he had hardly recollected that he was a physician at all. The sea and the wind had been Sally's real physicians, and the baby's; and as for the other two, in the happy quartette, had they needed a physician? Perhaps; but no physician was there for them.

"Certainly! certainly!" he stammered, "it will be safe;" and his face grew redder and redder, as he spoke. Hetty looked at him in honest amazement. She could put but one interpretation on his manner.

"Why, there is no need of our going yet, if it isn't best. Don't look so! Sally can stay here all summer if it will do her good."

"You misunderstood me, Miss Gunn," said the doctor, now himself again. "It will really be perfectly safe for Mrs. Little to go home. She is entirely well."

"What did you mean then?" said Hetty, looking him straight in the eye with honest perplexity in her face. "You looked as if you didn't think it best to go."

"No, Miss Gunn," replied Dr. Eben. "I looked as if I did not want to go. It has been so pleasant here: that was all."

"Oh," said Hetty, in a relieved tone, "was that it? I feel just so, too: it has been delightful; it is the only real play-spell I ever had in my life. But for all that I'm really impatient to get home: they need me on the farm; the men have not been doing just as they ought to. Jim Little is all right when I'm there; but they take advantage of him when I'm away. I really must get home before haying. I think we must certainly go some day next week."

Dr. Eben was just going over to town for the letters. As he walked slowly down to the beach, he said to himself:

"Haying! By Jove!" and this was pretty much all he thought during the whole of the hour that he spent in rowing to and from the Safe Haven wharf. "Haying!" he ejaculated again, and again. "What a woman that is! I believe if we were all dead, she'd have just as keen an eye to that haying!"

By "we all" in that sentence of his soliloquy, Dr. Eben really meant "I." He was beginning to be half aware of a personal unhappiness, because Hetty showed no more consciousness of his existence. Her few words this morning about returning home had produced startling results in his mind; like those a chemist sometimes sees in his crucible, when, on throwing in a single drop of some powerful agent, he discovers by its instantaneous and infallible test, the presence of things he had not suspected were there. Dr. Eben Williams clenched his hands as he paced up and down the beach. He did not wish to love Hetty Gunn. He did not approve of loving Hetty Gunn; but love her he did with the whole strength of his soul. In this one brief hour, he had become aware of it. What would be its result, in vain he tried to conjecture. One moment, he said to himself that it was not in Hetty's nature to love any man; the next moment, with a lover's inconsistency, he reproached himself for a thought so unjust to her: one moment, he rated himself soundly for his weakness, and told himself sternly that it was plain Hetty cared no more for him than she did for one of her farm laborers; the next moment, he fell into reverie full of a vague and hopeful recalling of all the kind and familiar things she had ever done or said. The sum and substance of his meditations was, however, that nothing should lead him to commit the folly of asking Hetty to marry him, unless her present manner toward him changed.

"I dare say she would laugh in my face," thought he; "I don't know but that she would in any man's face who should ask her," and, armed and panoplied in this resolution, Dr. Eben walked up to the spot where Hetty sat under one of the old Balm of Gilead trees sewing, with the baby in its cradle at her feet. It was still early morning: the Safe Haven spires shone in the sun, and the little fishing schooners were racing out to sea before the wind. This was one of the prettiest sights from the beach at "The Runs." Every morning scores of little fishing vessels came down the river, shot past like arrows, and disappeared beyond the bar. At night they came home again slowly; sometimes with their sails cross-set, which made them look like great white butterflies skimming the water. Hetty never wearied of watching them: still pictures never wholly pleased her. The things in nature which had motion, evident aim, purpose, arrested her eye, and gave her delight.

"I haven't learned to sail a boat yet, after all," she said regretfully, as the doctor came up. "Only see how lovely they are. I wish I could buy this whole place, and carry it home. I think we will all come here again next summer."

"Not all," said Dr. Eben; "I shall not be here with you."

"No, I hope not," replied Hetty, unconsciously.

Dr. Eben laughed outright: her tone was so unaffectedly honest.

"Oh, you know what I mean," exclaimed Hetty, "I mean, I hope Sally will not have to bring you as a physician. Of course, there is nothing to hinder your coming here at any time, if you like," she added, in a kindly but indifferent tone.

"But I should not want to come alone," said the doctor.

"No," said Hetty, reflectively. "It would be dull, I shouldn't like it myself, to be here all alone. The sea is the loneliest of things in the universe, I think. The fields and the woods and the hills all look as if they had good fellowship with each other perpetually; but the great, blank, bare sea, looks for ever alone; and sometimes the waves seem to me to run up on the shore as fiercely as starved wolves leaping on prey!"

"Not on this little comfortable beach, though," said Dr. Eben.

"Oh, no!" replied Hetty, "I did not mean such sea-shore as this. But even here, I should find it sad if I were alone."

"All places are sad if one is alone, Miss Gunn," replied the doctor, in a pensive tone, rare with him.

Hetty turned a surprised glance at him, and did not speak for a moment. Then she said:

"Yes; but nobody need be alone: there are always plenty of people to take into one's house. If you are lonely, why don't you get somebody to live with you, or you might be married," she added, in as purely matter-of-fact a tone, as she would have said, "you might take a journey," or "you might build on a wing to your house."

This suggestion sounded oddly enough, coming so soon from the lips of the woman whom the doctor had just been ardently wishing he could marry; but its cool and unembarrassed tone was sufficient to corroborate his utmost disheartenment.

"Ah!" he thought, "I knew she didn't care any thing for me!" and he fell into a silent brown study which Hetty did not attempt to break. This was one among her many charms to Dr. Eben, that she was capable of sitting quietly by a person's side for long intervals of silence. The average woman, when she is in the company of even a single person, seems to consider herself derelict in duty, if conversation is not what she calls "kept up;" an instinctive phrase, which, by its universal use, is the bit terest comment on its own significance. Men have no such feeling. Two men will sit by each other's side, it may be for hours, in silence, and feel no derogation from good comradeship. Why should not women? The answer is too evident. Women have a perpetual craving to be recognized, to be admired; and a large part of their ceaseless chatter is no more nor less than a surface device to call your attention to them; as little children continually pull your gown to make you look at them. Hetty was incapable of this. She was a vivacious talker when she had any thing to say; but a most dogged holder of her tongue when she had not. In this instance she had nothing to say, and she did not speak: the doctor had so much to say that he did not speak, and they sat in silence till the shrill bell from the farm-house door called them to dinner. As they walked slowly up to the house, the doctor said:

"You don't wonder that I hate to go away from this lovely place, do you, Miss Gunn?"

Any other woman but Hetty would have felt something which was in his tone, though not in his words. But Hetty answered bluntly:

"Yes, I do wonder; it is very lovely here: but I should think you'd want to be at work; I do.

I think we've had play-spell enough; for, after all, it hasn't been any thing but play-spell for you and me."

"Now she despises me," thought poor Dr. Eben. "She hasn't any tolerance in her, anyhow," and he was grave and preoccupied all through dinner.

VII.

IT was settled that they should set out for home a week from that day. "Only seven days left," said the doctor. "What can I do in that time?"

Never was man so baffled in attempts to woo. Hetty saw nothing, heard nothing, understood nothing; unwittingly she defeated every project he made for seeing her alone; unconsciously she chilled and dampened and arrested every impulse he had to speak to her, till Dr. Eben's temper was tried as well as his love. Sally, the baby, the nurse, all three, were simply a wall of protection around Hetty. Her eyes, her ears, her hands were full; and as for her heart and soul, they were walled about even better than her body. Nothing can be such a barrier to love's approach as an honest nature's honest unconsciousness. Dr. Eben was wellnigh beside himself. The days flew by. He had done nothing, gained nothing. How he cursed his folly in having let two whole months slip away, before he found out that he loved this woman, whom now he could no more hope to impress in a few hours' time than a late afternoon sun might think to melt an iceberg.

"It would take a man a lifetime to make her understand that he loved her," groaned the doctor, "and I've only got two days;" and more than ever his anxiety deepened as he wondered whether, after they returned home, she would allow him to continue these friendly and familiar relations. This uncertainty led to a most unfortunate precipitation on his part. The night before they were to go, he found Hetty at sunset sitting under the trees, and looking dreamily out to sea. Her attitude and her look were pensive. He had never seen such an expression on Hetty's face or figure, and it gave him a warmer yearning towards her than he had ever yet dared to let himself feel. It was just time for the lamp in the lighthouse to be lit, and Hetty was watching for it. As the doctor approached her, she said, "I am waiting for the lighthouse light to flash out. I like so to see its first ray. It is like seeing a new planet made." Dr. Eben sat down by her side, and they both waited in silence for the light. The whole western and southern sky glowed red; a high wind had been blowing all day, and the water was covered with foamy white caps; the tall, slender obelisk of the lighthouse stood out black against the red sky, and the shining waves leaped up and broke about its base. But all was quiet in the sheltered curve of the beach on which Hetty and Dr. Eben were sitting: the low surf rose and fell as gently as if it had a tide of its own, which no storm could touch. Presently the bright light flashed from the tower, shone one moment on the water of the river's mouth, then was gone.

"Now it is lighting the open sea," said Hetty. In a few moments more the lantern had swung round, and again the bright rays streamed towards the beach, almost reaching the shore.

"And now it is lighting us," said Dr. Eben: "I wish it were as easy to get light upon one's path in life, as it is to hang a lantern in a tower."

Hetty laughed.

"Are you often puzzled?" she asked lightly.

"No," said the doctor, "I never have been, but I am now."

"What about?" asked Hetty, innocently: "I don't see what there is to puzzle you here."

"You, Miss Gunn," stoutly answered Dr. Eben, feeling as if he were taking a header into unfathomed waters.

"Me!" exclaimed Hetty, in a tone of utmost surprise. "Why, what do you mean?"

Dr. Eben hesitated a single instant. He had not intended to do this thing, but the occasion had been too much for him. "I may as well do it first as last," he said; "she can but refuse me:" and, in a very few manly words, Dr. Eben Williams straightway asked Hetty Gunn to marry him. He was not prepared for what followed, although in a soliloquy, only a few days before, he had predicted it to himself. Hetty laughed merrily, unaffectedly, in his very face.

"Why, Dr. Williams!" she said, "you can't know what you're saying. You can't want to marry me: I'm not the sort of woman men want to marry"—

He interrupted her. His voice was husky with deep feeling.

"Miss Gunn," he said, "I implore you not to speak in this way. I do know what I am saying, and I do love you with all my heart."

"Nonsense," answered Hetty in the kindliest of tones; "of course you think you do: but it is only because you have been shut up here two whole months, with nothing else to do but fancy that you were in love. I told you it was time we went home. Don't say any thing more about it. I'll promise you to forget it all," and Hetty laughed again, a merry little laugh. A sharp suspicion crossed the doctor's mind that she was coquetting with him. In a constrained tone he said:

"Miss Gunn, do you really wish me to understand that you reject me?"

"Not at all," said Hetty, gayly. "I wish you to understand that I haven't permitted you to offer yourself. I have simply assured you that you are mistaken: you'll see it for yourself as soon as we get home. Do you suppose I shouldn't know if you were really in love with me?"

"I didn't know it myself till a week ago," replied Dr. Eben: "I did not understand myself. I never loved any woman before."

"And no man ever asked me to marry him before," answered the honest Hetty, like a child, and with an amused tone in her voice. "It is very odd, isn't it?"

Dr. Eben was confounded. In spite of himself, he felt the contagion of Hetty's merry and unsentimental view of the situation; and it was with a trace of obstinacy rather than of a lover's pain in his tones that he continued:

"But, Miss Gunn, indeed you must not make

light of this matter in this way. It is not treating me fairly. With all the love of a man's heart I love you, and have asked you to be my wife: are you sure that you could not love me?"

"I don't really think I could," said Hetty; "but I shall not try, because I am sure you are mistaken. I am too old to be married, for one thing: I shall be thirty-seven in the fall. That's reason enough, if there were no other. A man can't fall in love with a woman after she's as old as that."

Dr. Eben laughed outright. He could not help it.

"There!" said Hetty, triumphantly; "that's right; I like to hear you laugh now; for goodness' sake, let's forget all this. I will, if you will; and we will be all the better friends for it perhaps. At any rate, you'll be all the more friend to me for having saved you from making such a blunder as thinking you were in love with me."

Dr. Eben was on the point of persisting farther; but he suddenly thought to himself:

"I'd better not: I might make her angry. I'll take the friendship platform for the present: that is some gain."

"You will permit me then to be your friend, Miss Gunn," he said.

"Why, certainly," said Hetty, in a matter-of-fact way: "I thought we were very good friends now."

"But you recollect, you distinctly told me I was to come only as physician to Mrs. Little," retorted the doctor.

Hetty colored: the darkness sheltered her.

"Oh! that was a long time ago," she said in a remorseful tone: "I should be very ungrateful if I had not forgotten that."

And with this Dr. Eben was forced to be contented. When he thought the whole thing over, he admitted to himself that he had fared as well as he had a right to expect, and that he had gained a very sure vantage, in having committed the loyal Hetty to the assertion that they were friends. He half dreaded to see her the next morning, lest there should be some change, some constraint in her manner; not a shade of it. He could have almost doubted his own recollections of the evening before, if such a thing had been possible, so absolutely unaltered was Hetty's treatment of him. She had been absolutely honest in all she said: she did honestly believe that his fancied love for her was a sentimental mistake, a caprice born of idleness and lack of occupation, and she did honestly intend to forget the whole thing, and to make him forget it. And so they went back to the farm, where the summer awaited them with overflowing harvests of every thing, and Hetty's hands were so full that very soon she had almost ceased to recollect the life at "The Runs." Sally and the baby were strong and well. The whole family seemed newly glad and full of life. All odd hours they could snatch from work, Old Cæsar and Nan roamed about in the sun, following the baby, as his nurse carried him in her arms. He had been christened Abraham Gunn Little; poor James Little having persistently refused to let his own name be given to the child, and Hetty having been cordially willing to give her father's. To speak to a baby as Abraham was manifestly impossible, and the little fellow was called simply "Baby" month after month, until, one day, one of Norah's toddlers, who could not speak plain, hit upon a nickname so fortunate that it was at once adopted by everybody. "Raby," little Mike called him, by some original process of compounding "Abraham" and "Baby;" and "Raby" he was from that day out. He was a beautiful child: his mother's blue eyes, his father's dark hair, and a skin like a ripe peach, but not over fair, — made a combination of color which was rarely lovely. He was a joyous child, as joyous as if no shadow had ever rested on his mother's heart. Sally watched him day by day with delight; but the delight was never wholly free from pain: the wound she had received, the wound she had inflicted on herself, could never wholly heal. A deep, moral hurt must for ever leave its trace, as surely as a deep wound in a man's flesh must leave its scar. It is of no use for us to think to evade this law; neither is it a law wholly of retribution. The scar on the flesh is token of nature's process of healing: so is the scar of a perpetual sorrow, which is left on a soul which has sinned and repented. Sally and Jim were leading healthful and good lives now; and each day brought them joys and satisfactions: but their souls were scarred; the fulness of joy which might have been theirs they could never taste. And the loss fell where it could never be overlooked for a moment, — on their joy in their child. In the very holiest of holies, in the temple of the mother's heart, stood for ever a veiled shape, making ceaseless sin-offering for the past.

As the winter set in, an anxiety fell on the family which had passed so sunny a summer. With the first sharp cold winds, little Raby developed a tendency to croup. Neither Sally nor Hetty had ever seen a case of this terrible and alarming disease; and, in Raby's first attack of it, they had both thought the child dying. Now was Doctor Eben brought again into close and intimate relations with Hetty. During the months of the summer, he had, in spite of all his efforts, in spite of his frequent visits to her house, in spite of all Hetty's frank cordiality of manner, felt himself slowly slipping away from the vantage-ground he hoped he had gained with her. This was the result of two things, — one which he knew, and one which he did not dream of: the cause which he knew, was a very simple and evident one, Hetty's constant preoccupation. Hetty was a very busy woman: what with Raby, the farm, the house, her social relations with the whole village, she had never a moment of leisure. Often when Dr. Eben came to the house, he found her away; and often when he found her at home, she was called away before he had talked with her half an hour. The other reason, which, if Dr. Eben had only known it, would have more than comforted him for all he felt he had lost on the surface, was that Hetty, in the bottom of her heart, was slowly growing conscious that she cared a great deal about him.

No woman, whatever she may say and honestly mean, can entirely dismiss from her thoughts the memory of the words in which a man has told her he loves her. Especially is this true when those words are the first words of love which have ever been spoken to her. Morning and night, as Hetty came and went, in her brisk cheery way, in and out of the house and about the farm, she wore a new look on her face. The words, "I love you with all my heart," haunted her. She did not believe them any more now than before; but they had a very sweet sound. She was no nearer now than then to any impulse to take Dr. Williams at his word: nothing could be deeper implanted in a soul than the conviction was in Hetty's that no man was likely to love her. But she was no longer so sure that she herself could not love. Vague and wistful reveries began to interrupt her activity. She would stand sometimes, with her arms folded, leaning on a stile, and idly watching her men at work, till they wondered what had happened to their mistress. She lost a little of the color from her cheeks, and the full moulded lines of her chin grew sharper.

"Faith, an' Miss Hetty's goin' off, sooner'n she's any right to," said Mike to Norah one day.

"What puts such a notion in your head thin, Mike?" retorted Norah, "sure she's as foine a craythur as's in all the county, an' foiner too."

"Foine enough, but I say for all that that she's a goin' off in her looks mighty fast," replied the keen-eyed Mike. "You don't think she'd be a pinin' for anybody, do you?"

Norah gave a hearty Irish laugh.

"Miss Hetty a pinin'!" she repeated over and over with bursts of merriment:

"Ah, but yez are all alike, ye men. Miss Hetty a pinin'! I'd like to see the man Miss Hetty wud pine fur."

Mike and Norah were both right. There was no "pining" in Hetty's busy and sensible soul; but there had been planted in it a germ of new life, whose slow quickening and growth were perplexing and disturbing elements: not as yet did she recognize them; she only felt the disturbance, and its link with Dr. Eben was sufficiently clear to make her manner to him undergo an indefinable change. It was no less cordial, no less frank: you could not have said where the change was; but it was there, and he felt it. He ought to have understood it and taken heart. But he was ignorant like Hetty, only felt the disturbance, and taking counsel of his fears believed that things were going wrong. Sometimes he would stay away for many days, and then watch closely Hetty's manner when they met. Never a trace of resentment or even wonder at his absence. Sometimes he would go there daily for an interval; never a trace of expectation or of added familiarity. But now things were changed. Little Raby's illness seemed to put them all back where they were during the days of the sea-side idyl. Now the doctor felt himself again needed. Both Hetty and Sally lived upon his words, even his looks. Again and again the child's life seemed hanging in even balances, and it was with a gratitude almost like that they felt to God that the two women blessed Dr. Eben for his recovery. Night after night, the three watched by the baby's bed, listening to his shrill and convulsive breathings.

Morning after morning, Dr. Eben and Hetty went together out of the chamber, and stood in the open door-way, watching the crimson dawn on the eastern hills. At such times, the doctor felt so near Hetty that he was repeatedly on the point of saying again the words of love he had spoken six months before. But a great fear deterred him.

"If she refuses me once more, that would settle it for ever," he said to himself, and forced the words back.

One morning after a night of great anxiety and fear, they left Sally's room while it was yet dark. It was bitterly cold; the winter stars shone keen and glittering in the bleak sky. Hetty threw on a heavy cloak, and opening the hall-door, said:

"Let us go out into the cold air; it will do us good."

Silently they walked up and down the piazza. The great pines were weighed down to the ground by masses of snow. Now and then, when the wind stirred the upper branches, avalanches slid noiselessly off, and built themselves again into banks below. There was no moon, but the starlight was so brilliant that the snow crystals glistened in it. As they looked at the sky, a star suddenly fell. It moved very slowly, and was more than a minute in full sight.

"One light-house less," said Dr. Eben.

"Oh," exclaimed Hetty, "what a lovely idea! who said that? Who called the stars light-houses?"

"I forget," said the doctor; "in fact I think I never knew; I think it was an anonymous little poem in which I saw the idea, years ago. It struck me at the time as being a singularly happy one. I think I can repeat a stanza or two of it."

GOD'S LIGHT-HOUSES.

When night falls on the earth, the sea
    From east to west lies twinkling bright
With shining beams from beacons high,
    Which send afar their friendly light.

The sailors' eyes, like eyes in prayer,
    Turn unto them for guiding ray:
If storms obscure their radiance,
    The great ships helpless grope their way.

When night falls on the earth, the sky
    Looks like a wide, a boundless main;
Who knows what voyagers sail there?
    Who names the ports they seek and gain?

Are not the stars like beacons set,
    To guide the argosies that go
From universe to universe,
    Our little world above, below?

On their great errands solemn bent,
    In their vast journeys unaware
Of our small planet's name or place
    Revolving in the lower air.

Oh thought too vast! oh thought too glad:
    An awe most rapturous it stirs.
From world to world God's beacons shine:
    God means to save his mariners!

Hetty was silent. The mention of light-houses had carried her thoughts back to that last night at "The Runs," when, with Dr. Eben by her side, she had watched the great revolving light in the stone tower on the bar.

Dr. Eben was thinking of the same thing; he wondered if Hetty were not: after a few moments' silence, he became so sure of it that he said:

"You have not forgotten that night, have you?"

"Oh, no!" replied Hetty, in a low voice.

"I should like to think that you did not wish to forget it," said the doctor, in a tender tone.

"Oh, don't, please don't say any thing about it," exclaimed Hetty, in a tone so full of emotion, that Dr. Eben's heart gave a bound of joy. In that second, he believed that the time would come when Hetty would love him. He had never heard such a tone from her lips before. Her hand rested on his arm. He laid his upon it,—the first caressing touch he had ever dared to offer to Hetty; the first caressing touch which Hetty had ever received from hand of man.

"I will not, Hetty, till you are willing I should," he said. He had never called her "Hetty" before. A tumult filled Hetty's heart; but all she said was, in a most matter-of-fact tone:

"That's right! we must go in now. It is too cold out here."

Dr. Eben did not care what her words were: nature had revealed herself in a tone.

"I'll make her love me yet," he thought. "It won't take a great while either; she's beginning, and she doesn't know it." He was so happy that he did not know at first that Hetty had left him alone in front of the fire. When he found she had gone, he drew up a big arm-chair, sank back in its depths, put his feet on the fender, and fell to thinking how, by spring, perhaps, he might marry Hetty. In the midst of this lover-like reverie, he fell asleep in the most unlover-like way. He was worn out with his long night's watching. In a few minutes, Hetty came back with hot broth which she had prepared for him. Her light step did not rouse him. She stood still by his chair, looking down on his face. His clear-cut features, always handsome, were grand in sleep. The solemnity of closed eyes adds to a noble face something which is always very impressive. He stirred uneasily, and said in his sleep, "Hetty." A great wave of passionate feeling swept over her face, as, standing there, she heard this tender sound of her name on his unconscious lips.

"Oh what will become of me if I love him after all," she thought.

"Why not, why not?" answered her heart; wakened now and struggling for its craved and needed rights. "Why not, why not?" and no answer came to Hetty's mind.

Moving noiselessly, she set the broth on a low table by the doctor's side, covered him carefully with her own heavy cloak, and left the room. On the threshold, she turned back and looked again at his face. Her conscious thoughts were more than she could bear. In sudden impatience with herself, she exclaimed, "Pshaw! how silly I am!" and hastened upstairs, more like the old original Hetty than she had been for many days. Love could not enthrone himself easily in Hetty's nature: it was a rebellious kingdom. "Thirty-seven years old! Hetty Gunn, you're a goose," were Hetty's last thoughts as she fell asleep that night. But when she awoke the next morning, the same refrain, "Why not, why not?" filled her thoughts; and, when she bade Dr. Eben good-morning, the rosy color that mounted to her very temples gave him a new happiness.

Why prolong the story of the next few days? They were just such days as every man and every woman who has loved has lived through, and knows far better than can be said or sung. Love's beginnings are varied, and his final crises of avowal take individual shape in each individual instance: but his processes and symptoms of growth are alike in all cases; the indefinable delight, — the dreamy wondering joy, — the half avoidance which really means seeking, — the seeking which shelters itself under endless pleas, — the ceaseless questioning of faces, — the mute caresses of looks, and the eloquent caresses of tones, — are they not written in the books of the chronicles of all lovers? What matter how or when the crowning moment of full surrender comes? It came to Eben and Hetty, however, more suddenly at last than it often comes; came in a way so characteristic of them both, that perhaps to tell it may not be a sin, since we aim at a complete setting forth of their characters.

VIII.

FOR three days little Raby had been so ill that the doctor had not left the house day nor night, except for imperative calls from other patients. Each night the paroxysms of croup returned with great severity, and the little fellow's strength seemed fast giving way under them. Sally and Hetty, his two mothers, were very differently affected by the grief they bore in common. Sally was speechless, calm, almost dogged in her silence. When Dr. Eben trying to comfort her, said:

"Don't feel so, Mrs. Little: I think we shall pull the boy through all right." She looked up in his face, and shook her head, speaking no word. "I am not saying it merely to comfort you; indeed, I am not, Mrs. Little," said the doctor. "I really believe he will get well. These attacks of croup seem much worse than they really are."

"I don't know that it comforts me," replied

Sally, speaking very slowly. "I don't know that I want him to live; but I think perhaps he might be allowed to die easier, if I didn't need so much punishing. It is worse than death to see him suffer so."

"Oh, Mrs. Little! how can you think thus of God?" exclaimed the doctor. "He never treats us like that, any more than you could Raby."

"The minister at the Corners said so," moaned Sally. "He said it was till the third and fourth generations."

At such moments, Dr. Eben, in his heart, thought undevoutly of ministers. "A bruised reed, he will not break," came to his mind, often as he looked at this anguish-stricken woman, watching her only child's suffering, and morbidly believing that it was the direct result of her own sin. But Dr. Eben found little time to spare for his ministrations to Sally, when Hetty was in such distress. He had never seen any thing like it. She paced the house like a wounded lioness. She could not bear to stay in the room: all day, all night, she walked, walked, walked; now in the hall outside his door; now in the rooms below. Every few moments, she questioned the doctor fiercely: "Is he no better?" "Will he have another?" "Can't you do something more?" "Do you think there is a possibility that any other doctor might know something you do not?" "Shan't I send Cæsar over to Springton for Dr. Wilkes; he might think of something different?" These, and a thousand other such questions, Hetty put to the harassed and tortured Dr. Eben, over and over, till even his loving patience was wellnigh outworn. It was strengthened, however, by his anxiety for her. She did not eat; she did not drink; she looked haggard and feverish. This child had been to her from the day of his birth like her own: she loved him with all the pent-up forces of the great womanhood within her, which thus far had not found the natural outlet of its affections.

"Doctor," she would cry vehemently, "why should Raby die? God never means that any children should die. It is all our ignorance and carelessness; all the result of broken law. I've heard you say a hundred times, that it is a thwarting of God's plan whenever a child dies: why don't you cure Raby?"

"That is all true, Hetty," Dr. Eben would reply; "all very true: it is a thwarting of God's plan whenever any human being dies before he is fully ripe of old age. But the accumulated weight of generations of broken law is on our heads. Raby's little life has been all well ordered, so far as we can see; but, farther back, was something wrong or he would not be ill to-day. I have done my best to learn, in my little life, all that is known of methods of cure; but I have only the records of human ignorance to learn from, and I must fail again and again."

At last, on the fourth night, Raby slept: slept for hours, quietly, naturally, and with a gentle dew on his fair forehead. The doctor sat motionless by his bed and watched him. Sally, exhausted by the long watch, had fallen asleep on a lounge. The sound of Hetty's restless steps, in the hall outside, had ceased for some time. The doctor sat wondering uneasily where she had gone. She had not entered the room for more than an hour; the house grew stiller and stiller; not a sound was to be heard except little Raby's heavy breathing, and now and then one of those fine and mysterious noises which the timbers of old houses have a habit of making in the night-time. At last the lover got the better of the physician. Doctor Eben rose, and, stealing softly to the door, opened it as cautiously as a thief. All was dark.

"Hetty," he whispered. No answer. He looked back at Raby. The child was sleeping so soundly it seemed impossible that he could wake for some time. Doctor Eben groped his way to the head of the great stairway, and listened again. All was still.

"Hetty!" he called in a low voice, "Hetty!" No answer.

"She must have fallen asleep somewhere. She will surely take cold," the doctor said to himself; persuading his conscience that it was his duty to go and find her. Slowly feeling his way, he crept down the staircase. On the last step but one, he suddenly stumbled, fell, and barely recovered himself by his firm hold of the banisters, in time to hear Hetty's voice in a low imperious whisper:

"Good heavens, doctor! what do you want?"

"Oh Hetty! did I hurt you?" he exclaimed; "I never dreamed of your being on the stairs."

"I sat down a minute to listen. It was all so still in the room, I was frightened; and I must have been asleep a good while, I think, I am so cold," answered Hetty; her teeth beginning to chatter, and her whole body shaking with cold. "Why, how dark it is!," she continued; "the hall lamp has gone out: let me get a match."

But Dr. Eben had her two cold hands in his. "No, Hetty," he said, "come right back into the room: Raby is so sound asleep it will not wake him; and Sally is asleep too;" and he led her slowly towards the door. The night-lamp was burning low; its pale flame, and the flickering blaze of the big hickory logs on the hearth, made a glimmering twilight, whose fantastic lights and shadows shot out through the door-way into the gloom of the hall. As the first of these lights fell on Hetty's face, Dr. Eben started to see how white it was. Involuntarily he put his arm around her; and exclaimed "How pale you are, my poor Hetty! you are all worn out;" and, half supporting her with his arm, he laid his free hand gently on her hair.

Hetty was very tired; very cold; half asleep, and half frightened. She dropped her head on his shoulder for a second, and said: "Oh, what a comfort you are!"

The words had hardly left her lips when Doctor Eben threw both his arms around her, and held her tightly to his breast, whispering:

"Indeed, I will be a comfort to you, Hetty, if you will only let me."

Hetty struggled and began to speak.

"Hush! you will wake Raby," he said, and still held her firmly, looking unpityingly down into her face.

"You do love me, Hetty," he whispered triumphantly.

The front stick on the fire broke, fell in two blazing upright brands to right and left, and cast a sudden flood of light on the two figures in the door-way. Sally and Raby slept on. Still Doctor Eben held Hetty close, and looked with a keen and exultant gaze into her eyes.

"It isn't fair when I am so cold and sleepy," whispered Hetty, with a half twinkle in her half-open eyes.

"It is fair! It is fair! Any thing is fair! Every thing is fair," exclaimed the doctor in a whisper which seemed to ring like a shout, and he kissed Hetty again and again. Still Sally and Raby slept on: the hickory fire leaped up as in joy; and a sudden wind shook the windows.

Hetty struggled once more to free herself, but the arms were like arms of oak.

"Say that you love me, Hetty," pleaded the doctor.

"When you let me go, perhaps I will," whispered Hetty.

Instantly the arms fell; and the doctor stood opposite her in the door-way, his head bent forward and his eyes fixed on her face.

Hetty cast her eyes down. Words did not come. It would have been easier to have said them while she was held close to Doctor Eben's side. Suddenly, before he had a suspicion of what she was about to do, she had darted away, was lost in the darkness, and in a second more he heard her door shut at the farther end of the hall.

Dr. Eben laughed a low and pleasant laugh. "She might as well have said it," he thought: "she will say it to-morrow. I have won!" and he sank into the great white dimity-covered chair, at the head of Raby's bed, and looked into the fire. The very coals seemed to marshal themselves into shapes befitting his triumph: castles rose and fell; faces grew, smiled, and faded away smiling; roses and lilies and palms glowed ruby red, turned to silver, and paled into spiritual gray. The silence of the night seemed resonant with a very symphony of joy. Still Sally and Raby slept on. The boy's sweet face took each hour a more healthful tint; and, as Doctor Eben watched the blessed change, he said to himself:

"What a night! what a night! Two lives saved! Raby's and mine." As the morning drew near, he threw up the shades of the eastern window, and watched for the dawn. "I will see this day's sun rise," he said with a thrill of devout emotion; and he watched the horizon while it changed like a great flower calyx from gray to pearly yellow, from yellow to pale green, and at last, when it could hold back the day no longer, to a vast rose red with a golden sun in its centre.

IX.

THAT morning's light could have fallen on no happier house, the world over, than "Gunn's." A little child brought back to life, out of the gates of death; two hearts entering anew on life, through the gates of love; half a score of hearts, each glad in the gladness of each other, and in the gladness of all, — what a morning it was!

Doctor Eben and Hetty met at the head of the stairs.

"Oh, Hetty!" exclaimed the doctor.

"Well?" said Hetty, in a half-defiant tone, without looking up. He came nearer, and was about to kiss her.

She darted back, and lifting her eyes gave him a glance of such mingled love and reproof that he was bewildered.

"Why, Hetty, surely I may kiss you?" he exclaimed.

"I was asleep last night," she answered gravely,

"and you did very wrong," and without another word or look she passed on.

Doctor Eben was thoroughly angry.

"What does she mean?" he said to himself. "She needn't think I am to be played with like a boy;" and the doctor took his seat at the breakfast table, with a sterner countenance than Hetty had ever seen him wear. In a few moments she began to cast timid and deprecating looks at him. His displeasure hurt her indescribably. She had not intended to offend or repel him. She did not know precisely what she had intended: in fact she had not intended any thing. If the doctor had understood more about love, he would have known that all manifestations in Hetty at this time were simply like the unconscious flutterings of a bird in the hand in which it is just about to nestle and rest. But he did not understand, and when Hetty, following him into the hall, stood shyly by his side, and looking up into his face said inquiringly, "Doctor?" he answered her as she had answered him, a short time before, with the curt monosyllable, "Well?" His tone was curter than his words. Hetty colored, and saying gently, "No matter; nothing now," turned away. Her whole movement was so significant of wounded feeling that it smote Doctor Eben's heart. He sprang after her and laid his hand on her arm. " Hetty," he said, " do tell me what it was you were going to say; I did not mean to hurt your feelings : but I don't know what to make of you."

" Not—know—what—to—make—of —me ! " repeated Hetty, very slowly, in a tone of the intensest astonishment.

" You wouldn't say you loved me," replied the doctor, beginning to feel a little ashamed of himself.

Hetty's eyes were fixed on his now, with no wavering in their gaze. She looked at him, as if her life lay in the balance of what she might read in his face.

" Did you not know that I loved you before you asked me to say so ? " she said with emphasis. It was the doctor's turn now to color. He answered evasively :

" A man has no right to know that, Hetty, until a woman tells him so."

" Did you not think that I loved you," repeated Hetty, with the same emphasis, and a graver expression on her face.

Dr. Eben hesitated. Already, he felt a sort of fear of the incalculable processes and changes in this woman's mind. Would she be angry if he said, he had thought she loved him? Would she be sure to recognize any equivocation, and be angrier at that?

"Hetty," he said, taking her hand in his, "I did hope very strongly that you loved me, or else I should never have asked you to say so; but you ought to be willing to say so, if it be true. Think how many times I have said it to you."

Hetty's eyes did not leave his: their expression deepened until they seemed to darken and enlarge. She did not speak.

"Will you not say it now, Hetty?" urged the doctor.

"I can't," replied Hetty, and turned and walked slowly away. Presently she turned again, and walked swiftly back to him, and exclaimed:

"What do you suppose is the reason it is so hard for me to say it?"

Dr. Eben laughed. "I can't imagine, Hetty. The only thing that is hard for me, is not to keep saying it all the time."

Hetty smiled.

"There must be something wrong in me. I think I shall never say it. But I suppose"— She hesitated, and her eyes twinkled. "I suppose you might come to be very sure of it without my ever saying it?"

"I am sure of it now, you darling," exclaimed the doctor; and threw both his arms around her, and this time Hetty did not struggle.

When Welbury heard that Hetty Gunn was to marry Doctor Ebenezer Williams, there was a fine hubbub of talk. There was no half-way opinion in anybody's mind on the question. Everybody was vehement, one way or the other. All Doctor Eben's friends were hilarious; and the greater part of Hetty's were gloomy. They said, he was marrying her for her money; that Hetty was too old, and too independent in all her ways, to be married at all; that they would be sure to fall out quickly; and a hundred other things equally meddlesome and silly. But nobody so disapproved of the match that he stayed away from the wedding, which was the largest and the gayest wedding Welbury had ever seen. It went sorely against the grain with Hetty to invite Mrs. Deacon Little, but Sally entreated for it so earnestly that she gave way.

"I think if she once sees me with Raby in my arms, may be she'll feel kinder," said Sally. James Little had carried the beautiful boy, and laid him in his grandmother's arms many times; but, although she showed great tenderness toward the child, she had never yet made any allusion to Sally; and James, who had the same odd combination of weakness and tenacity which his mother had, had never broken the resolution which he had taken years ago: not to mention his wife's name in his mother's presence. Mrs. Little had almost as great a struggle with herself before accepting the invitation, as Hetty had had before giving it. Only her husband's earnest remonstrances decided her wavering will.

"It's only once, Mrs. Little," he said, "and there'll be such a crowd there that very likely you won't come near Sally at all. It don't look right for you to stay away. You don't know how much folks think of Sally now. She's been asked to the minister's to tea, she and James, with Hetty and the doctor, several times."

"She hain't, has she?" exclaimed Mrs. Little, quite thrown off her balance by this unexpected piece of news, which the wary deacon had been holding in reserve, as a good general holds his biggest guns, for some special occasion. "You don't tell me so! Well, well, folks must do as they like. For my part, I call that downright countenancing of iniquity. And I don't know how she could have the face to go, either. I must say, I have some curiosity to see how she behaves among folks."

"She's as modest and pretty in her ways as ever a girl could be," replied the deacon, who had learned during the past year to love his son's wife; "you won't have any call to be ashamed of her. I can tell you that much beforehand."

When Mrs. Little's eyes first fell upon her daughter-in-law, she gave an involuntary start. In the two years during which Mrs. Little had not seen her, Sally had changed from a timid, nervous, restless woman to a calm and dignified one. Very much of her old girlish beauty had returned to her, with an added sweetness from her sorrow. As she moved among the guests, speaking with gentle greeting to each, all eyes followed her with evident pleasure and interest. She wore a soft gray gown, which clung closely to her graceful figure: one pale pink carnation at her throat, and one in her hair, were her only ornaments. When Raby, with his white frock and blue ribbons, was in her arms, the picture was one which would have delighted an artist's eye. Mrs. Little felt a strange mingling of pride and irritation at what she saw. Very keenly James watched her: he hovered near her continually, ready to forestall any thing unpleasant or to assist any reconciliation. She observed this; observed, also, how his gaze followed each movement of Sally's: she understood it.

"You needn't hang round so, Jim," she said: "I can see for myself. If it's any comfort to you, I'll say that your wife's the most improved woman I ever saw; and I'm very glad on 't. But I ain't going to speak to her: I've said I won't, and I won't. People must lie on their beds as they make 'em."

James made no reply, but walked away. It seemed to him that, at that instant, a chord in his filial love snapped, and was for ever lost.

Moment by moment, Sally watched and waited for the recognition which never came. Bearing Raby in her arms, she passed and repassed, drawing as near Mrs. Little as she dared. "Surely she must see that nobody else here wholly despises me," thought the poor woman; and, whenever any one spoke with especial kindness to her, she glanced involuntarily to see if her mother-in-law were observing it. But all in vain. Mrs. Little's pale and weak blue eyes roamed everywhere, but never seemed to rest on Sally for a second. Gradually Sally comprehended that all her hopes had been unfounded, and a deep sadness settled on her expressive face. "It's no use," she thought, "she'll never speak to me in the world, if she won't to-night."

Even during the moments of the marriage

ceremony, Hetty observed the woe on Sally's countenance; and, strange as it may seem, — or would seem in any one but Hetty, — while the minister was making his most impressive addresses and petitions, she was thinking to herself: "The hard-hearted old woman! She hasn't spoken to Sally. I wish I hadn't asked her. I'll pay her off yet, before the evening is over."

After the ceremony was done, and the guests were crowding up to congratulate Hetty, she whispered to James:

"Bring Sally up here."

When Sally came, Hetty said:

"Stand here close to me, Sally. Don't go away."

Presently Deacon Little approached with Mrs. Little. Hetty kissed the good old man as heartily as if he had been her father; then, turning to Mrs. Little, she said in a clear voice:

"I am very glad to see you in my house at last, Mrs. Little. Have you seen Sally yet? She has been so busy receiving our friends, that I am afraid you have hardly had a chance to talk with her. Sally," she continued, turning and taking Sally by the hand, "I shall be at liberty now to attend to my friends, and you must devote yourself to Mrs. Little;" and, with the unquestioning gesture of an empress, Hetty passed Mrs. Little over into Sally's charge.

Nobody could read on Hetty's features at this moment any thing except most cordial good-will and the tender happiness of a bride; but her heart was fighting like a knight in a tournament for rescue of one beset, and she was inwardly saying: "If she dares to refuse speak to her now, I'll expose her before this whole roomful of people."

Mrs. Little did not dare. More than ever she dreaded Hetty at this moment, and her surprise and fear added something to her manner towards Sally which might almost have passed for eagerness, as they walked away together; poor Sally lifting one quick deprecating look at Hetty's smiling and inexorable face. Deacon Little hastily retreated to a corner, where he stood wiping his forehead, endeavoring not to look alarmed, and thinking to himself:

"Well, if Hetty don't beat all! What 'll Mrs. Little do now, I wonder?" And presently, as cautiously as a man stalking a deer, he followed the couple, and tried to judge, by the expression of his wife's face, how things were going. Things were going very well. Mrs. Little had, in common with all weak and obstinate persons, a very foolish fear of ever being supposed to be dictated to or controlled by anybody. She was distinctly aware that Hetty had checkmated her. She had strong suspicions that there might be others looking on who understood the game; and the only subterfuge left her, the only shadow of pretence of not having been outwitted, was to appear as if she were glad of the opportunity of talking with Sally. Sally's appealing affectionateness of manner went very far to make this easy. She had no resentment to conceal: all these years she had never blamed Jim's mother; she had only yearned to win her love, to be permitted to love her. She looked up in her face now, and said, as they walked on:

"Oh! I did so want to speak to you, but I did not dare to."

It consoled weak Mrs. Little, for her present consciousness of being very much afraid of Hetty, to hear that she herself had inspired a great terror in some one else; and she answered, condescendingly:

"I have always wished you well,"— she hesitated for a word, but finally said, — "Sally."

"Thank you," said Sally. "I know you did. I never wondered."

Mrs. Little was much appeased. She had not counted on such humility. At this moment they were met by the nurse, carrying Raby; and he was a fruitful subject of conversation. Presently he began to cry; and Sally, taking him in her arms, said, as if by a sudden inspiration, "I think I had better take him upstairs. Wouldn't you like to go up with me, and see what lovely rooms Hetty has given to Jim and me?"

The friendliness of the bedroom, the disarming presence of the baby, completed Mrs. Little's surrender; and when James Little, missing his wife, went to her room to seek her, he stood still on the threshold, mute with surprise. There sat his mother with Raby on her lap; Sally on her knees by an opened bureau-drawer, was showing her all Raby's clothes, and the two women's faces were aglow with pleasure. James stole in softly, came behind his mother, and kissed her as he had not kissed her since he was a boy. Neither of the three spoke; but little Raby crowed out a sudden and unexplained laugh, which seemed a fitting sign and seal of the happy moment, and set them all at ease. When Sally described the scene to Hetty, she said:

"Oh, I was so frightened when Jim came in! I thought he'd be sure to say something to his mother that would spoil every thing. But the Lord put it into Raby's head to go off in one of his great laughs at nothing, and that made us all laugh, and the first thing that came into my head was that verse, 'And a little child shall lead them.'"

"Dear me, Sally, does any thing happen that doesn't put you in mind of some verse in the Bible?" laughed Hetty.

"Not many things, Hetty," replied Sally. "Those years that I was alone all the time, I used to read it so much that it's always coming into my head now, whatever happens."

After the last guest had gone, Doctor Eben and Hetty stood alone before the blazing fire. Hetty was beautiful on this night: no white lace, no orange blossoms, to make the ill-natured sneer at the middle-aged bride attired like a girl; no useless finery to be laid away in chests and cherished as sentimental mementos of an occasion. A substantial heavy silk of a useful shade of useful gray was Hetty Gunn's wedding gown; and she wore on her breast and in her hair white roses, "which will do for my summer bonnets for years," Hetty had said, when she bought them.

But her cheeks were pink, her eyes bright, and

her brown curls lovelier than ever. Dr. Eben might well be pardoned the pride and delight with which he drew her to his side and exclaimed, "Oh, Hetty! are you really mine? How beautiful you look!"

"Do you think so?" said Hetty, taking a survey of herself in the old-fashioned glass slanted at a steep angle above the mantel-piece. "I don't. I hate fine gowns and flowers on me. If I 'd have dared to, I 'd have been married in my old purple."

"I shouldn't have cared," replied her husband. "But it is better as it is. Welbury people would have never left off talking, if you had done that."

They were a beautiful sight, the two, as they stood with their arms around each other, in the fire-light. Dr. Eben was tall and of a commanding figure; his head was almost too massive for even his broad shoulders; his black hair was wellnigh shaggy in its thickness; and his dark gray eyes looked out from under eyebrows which were like projecting eaves, and threw shadows on his cheeks below. Hetty's fair, rosy face, and golden-brown curls, were thrown out into relief by all this dark coloring so near, as a sunbeam is when it plays on a dark cloud. The rooms were full of the delicate fragance of apple blossoms. The corners were filled with them; the walls were waving with them. Sally had begged permission to have, for once, all the apple blossoms she desired; and, despite groans and grumblings from Mike, she had rifled the orchards.

"Faith, an' a good tin bushel she's taken off the russets," Mike said to Norah; "an' as for thim gillies yer was so fond of, there's none left to spake of on any o' the trees. Now if she'd er tuk thim old blue pearmain trees, I wouldn't have said a word. But, 'Oh no!' sez she, 'I must have all pink uns;' an' it was jest the pink uns that was our best trees; that's jest as much sinse as ye wimmin's got."

"Wull, thin, an' I'm thinkin' yer wouldn't have grudged Miss Hetty her own apples, if it was in barrls ye had 'em," replied the practical Norah, "an' I don't see where's the differ."

"Yer don't!" said Mike, angrily. "If it had ha plazed God to make a man o' yer, ye'd ha known more'n yer do;" and with this characteristically masculine shifting of his premises, Mike turned his back on Norah.

Neither Hetty nor Doctor Eben had ever heard that lovers should not wed in May; and, as they looked up at the great fragrant pink and white boughs on the walls, Hetty exclaimed:

"Nobody ought to be married except when apple-trees are in bloom. Nothing else could have been half so lovely in the rooms, and the fire-light makes them all the prettier. What a genius Sally has for arranging flowers. Who would have thought common stone jars could look so well?"

Sally had taken the largest sized gray stone jars she could buy in Welbury, and in these had set boughs six and seven feet long, looking like young trees. On the walls she had placed deep wooden boxes with shield-shaped fronts; these fronts were covered with gray lichens from the rocks; the rosy blossoms waved from out these boxes, looking as much at home as they did above the lichen-covered trunks of the trees in the orchard.

"Poor dear Sally!" Hetty continued, "she had a hard time the first part of the evening. That stony old woman wouldn't speak to her. But I took her in hand afterward. Did you observe?"

"Observe!" shouted Dr. Eben. "I should think so. You hardly waited till the minister had got through with us."

"L didn't wait till then," replied Hetty, demurely. "I was planning it all the while he was telling me about my duty to you. I didn't believe he could tell me much about that, anyway; and the duty that weighed on my mind most at that minute was my duty to Sally."

And thus, in the flickering fire-light and the apple-blossom fragrance, the two wedded lovers sat talking and dreaming, and taking joy of each other while the night wore on. There was no violent transition, no great change of atmosphere, in the beginnings of their wedded life. Dr. Eben had now lived so much at "Gunn's," that it seemed no strange thing for him to live there altogether. If it chafed him sometimes that it was Hetty's house and not his, Hetty's estate, Hetty's right and rule, he never betrayed it. And there was little reason that it should chafe him; for, from the day of Hetty Gunn's marriage, she was a changed woman in the habits and motives of her whole life. The farm was to her, as if it were not. All the currents of her being were set now in a new channel, and flowed as impetuously there as they had been wont to flow in the old ones. Her husband, his needs, his movements, were now the centre around which her fine and ceaseless activity revolved. There was not a trace of sentimental expression to this absorption. A careless observer might have said that her manner was deficient in tenderness; that she was singularly chary of caresses and words of love. But one who saw deeper would observe that not the smallest motion of the doctor's escaped her eye; not his lightest word failed to reach her ear; and every act of hers was planned with either direct or indirect reference to him. In his absence, she was preoccupied and uneasy; in his presence, she was satisfied, at rest, and her face wore a sort of quiet radiance hard to describe, but very beautiful to see. As for Dr. Eben, he thought he had entered into a new world. Warmly as he had loved and admired Hetty, he had not been prepared for these depths in her nature. Every day he said to her, "Oh, Hetty, Hetty! I never knew you. I did not dream you were like this." She would answer lightly, laughingly, perhaps almost brusquely; but intense feeling would glow in her face as a light shines through glass; and often, when she turned thus lightly away from him, there were passionate tears in her eyes. It very soon became her habit to drive with him wherever he went. Old Doctor Tuthill had died some months before, and now the county circuit was Doctor Eben's. His love of his profession was a passion, and nothing now stood in the way of his gratifying it to the utmost. Books, journals, all poured in upon him. Hetty would have liked to be omniscient that she might procure for him all he could desire. Every morning they might be seen dashing over the country with a pair of fleet, strong gray horses. In the afternoon, they drove a pair of black ponies for visits nearer home. Sometimes, while the doctor paid his visits, Hetty sat in the carriage; and, when she suspected that he had fallen into some discussion not relative to the patient's case, she would call out merrily, with tones clear and ringing enough to penetrate any walls: "Come, come, doctor! we must be off." And the doctor would spring to his feet, and run hastily, saying: "You see I am under orders too: my doctor is waiting outside." Under the seat, side by side with the doctor's medicine case, always went a hamper which Hetty called "the other medicine case;" and far the more important it was of the two. Many a poor patient got well by help of Hetty's soups and jellies and good bread. Nothing made her so happy as to have the doctor come home, saying: "I've got a patient to-day that we must feed to cure him." Then only, Hetty felt that she was of real help to her husband: of any other help that she might give him Hetty was still incredulous; intangible things were a little out of Hetty's range. Even her great and passionate love had not fully opened her eyes to all love's needs and expressions. All that it meant to her was a perpetual doing, ministration, a compelling of the happiness of the loved object. And here, as everywhere else in her life, she was fully content only when there was something evident and ready to be done. If her husband had taken the same view of love, — had insisted on perpetual ministerings to her in tangible forms, — she would have been bewildered and uncomfortable; and would, no doubt, have replied most illogically: "Oh, don't be taking so much trouble about me. I can take care of myself; I always have." But Doctor Eben was in no danger of disturbing Hetty in this way. Without being consciously a selfish man, he had a temperament to which acceptance came easy. And really Hetty left him no time, no room, for any such manifestations towards her, even had they been spontaneously natural. Moreover, Hetty was a most difficult person for anybody to help in any way. She never seemed to have needs or wants: she was always well, brisk, cheery, prepared for whatever occurred. There really seemed to be nothing to do for Hetty but to kiss her; and that Doctor Eben did most heartily, and of persistence; and Hetty liked it better than any thing in this world. With his whole heart and strength, Eben Williams loved his wife; and he loved her better and better, day by day. But she herself, by her peculiar temperament, her habits of activity, and disinterestedness, made it, in the outset, out of the question that any man living with her as her husband should ever fully learn a husband's duties and obligations.

X.

AND now we shall pass over an interval of eight years in the history of "Gunn's." For it is only the "strange history" of Eben and Hetty that was to be told in this story, and in these years' history was nothing strange; unless, indeed, it might be said that they were strangely happy years. The household remained unchanged, except that there were three more babies in Mike's cottage, and Hetty had been obliged to build on another room for him. Old Nan and Cæsar still reigned. Cæsar's head was as white and tight-curled as the fleece of a pet lamb. He was now a shining light in the Methodist meeting; but he had not yet broken himself of his oaths. "Damn — bress de Lord" was still heard on occasion: but everybody, even Nan, had grown so used to it that it did not pass for an oath; and, no doubt, even the recording angel had long since ceased to put it down.

James Little and his wife were now as much a part of the family as if they had had the old Squire's blood in their veins; and nobody thought about the old time of their disgrace, — nobody but Jim and Sally themselves. From their thoughts it was never absent, when they looked on the beautiful, joyous face of Raby. He had grown beyond his years, and looked like a boy of twelve. He was manly, frank, impulsive; a child after Hetty's own heart, and much more like her than he was like his father or his mother. It was a question, also, if he did not love her more than he loved either of his parents: all his hours with her were unclouded; over his intercourse with them, there always hung the undefined cloud of an unexpressed sadness.

Hetty was changed. Her hair was gray; her fair skin weather-beaten; and the fine wrinkles around the corners of her merry eyes radiated like the spokes of a wheel. She had looked young at thirty-seven; she looked old at forty-five. The phlegmatic and lazy sometimes seem to keep their youth better than the sanguine and active. It is a cruel thing that laughter should age a woman's face almost as much as weeping; but it does. Sunny as

Hetty's face was, it had come to have a look older than it ought, simply because the kindly eyes had so often twinkled and half closed in merry laughter.

Time had dealt more kindly with Doctor Eben. He was a handsomer man at forty-one than he had been at thirty-three: the eight years had left no other trace upon him. Face, figure, step, all were as full of youth and vigor as upon the day when Hetty first met him walking down the pine-shaded road. The precise moment when the first pang of consciousness of the discrepancy between her husband's looks and her own entered Hetty's mind would be hard to determine. It began probably in some thoughtless jest of her own, or even of his; for, in his absolute loyalty of love, his unquestioning and long-established acceptance of their relation as a perfect one, it would never have crossed Doctor Eben's mind that Hetty could possibly care whether she looked older or younger than he. He never thought about her age at all: in fact, he could not have told either her age or his own with exactness; he was curiously forgetful of such matters. He did not see the wrinkles around her eyes. He did not know that her skin was weather-beaten, her figure less graceful, her hair fast turning gray. To him she was simply "Hetty:" the word meant as it always had meant, fulness of love, delight, life. Doctor Eben was a man of that fine fibre of organic loyalty, to which there is not possible, even a temptation to forsake or remove from its object. Men having this kind of uprightness and loyalty, rarely are much given to words or demonstrations of affection. To them love takes its place, side by side with the common air, the course of the sun, the succession of days and nights, and all other unquestioned and unalterable things in the world. To suggest to such a man the possibility of lessening in his allegiance to a wife, is like proposing to him to overthrow the whole course of nature. He simply cannot conceive of such a thing; and he has no tolerance for it. He is by the very virtue of his organic structure incapable of charity for men who sin in that way. There are not many such men, but the type exists; and well may any woman felicitate herself to whom it is given to rest her life on such sure foundations. If there be some lack of the daily manifestations of tenderness, the ready word, the ever-present caress, she may recollect that these are often the first fruits of a passion whose early way-side harvest will be scorched and shrivelled as soon as the sun is high; while the seed which bringeth forth a hundred, nay a thousand fold, of true grain, sleeps in long silence, and grows up noiseless and slow.

Doctor Eben did not know that he was in many small ways an unloverlike husband. He did not know that his absorption in his professional studies made him often seem unaware of Hetty's presence for hours together, when she was watching and waiting for a word. He did not know that he sometimes did not hear when she spoke, and did not answer when he heard. He did not know a hundred things which he would have known, if he had been a less upright and loyal man, and if Hetty had been a less unselfish woman. Neither did Hetty know any of these things, or note them, until the poisoned consciousness awoke in her mind that she was fast growing old, and her face was growing less lovely. This was the first germ of Hetty's unhappiness. It had been very hard for her in the beginning to believe herself loved: now all her old incredulity returned with fourfold strength; and now it was not met as then by constant and vehement evidence to conquer it. Here again, had Hetty been like other women, she might have been spared her suffering. Had it been possible for her to demand, to even invite, she would have won from her husband, at any instant, all that her anxiety could have asked; but it was not possible. She simply went on silently, day after day, watching her husband more intently; keeping record, in her morbid feeling, of every moment, every look, every word which she misapprehended. Beyond this morbidness of misapprehension, there was no other morbidness in Hetty's state. She did not pine or grieve; she only began slowly to wonder what she could do for Eben now. Her sense of loss and disappointment, in that she had borne him no children, began to weigh more heavily upon her. "If I were mother of his children," she said to herself, "it would not make so much difference if I did grow old and ugly. He would have the children to give him pleasure." "I don't see what there is left for me to do," she said again and again. Sometimes she made pathetic attempts to change the simplicity of her dress. "Perhaps if I wore better clothes, I should look younger," she thought. But the result was not satisfactory. Her severe style had always been so essentially her own that any departure from it only made her look still more altered. All this undercurrent of annoyance and distress added continually to the change in her face: gradually its expression grew more grave; she smiled less frequently; had fits of abstraction and reverie, which she had never been known to have before.

In a vague way, Doctor Eben observed these, and wondered what Hetty was thinking about; but he never asked. Often they drove for a whole day together, without a dozen words being spoken; but the doctor was buried in meditations upon his patients, and did not dislike the silence. Hetty did not realize that the change here was more in her than in him: in the old days it had been she who talked, not the doctor; now that she was silent, he went on with his trains of thought undisturbed, and was as content as before, for she was by his side. He felt her presence perpetually, even when he gave no sign of doing so.

Many months went by in this way, a summer, a winter, part of a spring, and Hetty's forty-fifth birthday came, and found her a seriously unhappy woman. Yet, strange to say, nobody dreamed of it. So unchanged was the external current of her life: such magnificent self-control had she, and such absolute disinterestedness.

Little Raby was the only one who ever had a consciousness that things were not right. He was Hetty's closest comrade and companion now. All the hours that she did not spend driving with the doctor (and she drove with him less now than had been her custom) she spent with Raby. They took long rambles together, and long rides, Raby being already an accomplished and fearless little rider. By the subtle instinct of a loving child, Raby knew that "Aunt Hetty" was changed. A certain something was gone out of the delight they used to take together. Once, as they were riding, he exclaimed:

"Aunt Hetty, you haven't spoken for ever so long! What's the matter? you don't talk half so much as you used to."

And Hetty, conscience-stricken, thought to herself: "Dear me, how selfish it makes one to be unhappy! Here I am, letting it fall on this dear, innocent darling. I ought to be ashamed." But she answered gayly:

"Oh, Raby! aunty is growing old and stupid, isn't she? She must look out, or you'll get tired of her."

"I shan't either: you're the nicest aunty in the whole world," cried Raby. "You ain't a bit old; but I wish you'd talk."

Then and there, Hetty resolved that never again should Raby have occasion to think thus; and he never did. Before long he had forgotten all about this conversation, and all was as before. This was in May. One day, in the following June, as Hetty and the doctor were driving through Springton, he said suddenly:

"Oh, Hetty! I want you to come in with me at one place this morning. There is the most perfectly beautiful creature there I ever saw,— the oldest daughter of a Methodist minister who has just come here to preach. Poor child! she cannot sit up, or turn herself in bed; but she is an angel, and has the face of one, if ever a human creature had. They are very poor and we must help them all we can. I have great hopes of curing the child, if she can be well fed. It is a serious spinal disease, but I believe it can be cured."

When Hetty first looked on the face of Rachel Barlow, she said in her heart: "Eben was right. It is the face of an angel;" and when she heard Rachel's voice, she added, "and the voice also." Some types of spinal disease seem to have a marvellously refining effect on the countenance; producing an ethereal clearness of skin, and brightness of eye, and a spiritual expression, which are seen on no other faces. Rachel Barlow was a striking instance of this almost abnormal beauty. As her fair face looked up at you from her pillow, your impulse was to fall on your knees. Not till she smiled did you feel sure she was human; but when she smiled, the smile was so winningly warm, you forgot you had thought her an angel. For two years she had not moved from her bed, except as she was lifted in the strong arms of her father. For two years she had not been free from pain for a moment. Often the pain was so severe that she fainted. And yet her brow was placid, unmarked by a line, and her face in repose as serene as a happy child's.

Doctor Eben and Hetty sat together by the bed.

"Rachel," said the doctor, "I have brought my wife to help cure you. She is as good a doctor as I am." And he turned proudly to Hetty.

Rachel gazed at her earnestly, but did not speak. Hetty felt herself singularly embarrassed by the gaze.

"I wish I could help you," she said; "but I think my husband will make you well."

Rachel colored.

"I never permit myself to hope for it," she replied. "If I did, I should be discontented at once."

"Why! are you contented as it is?" exclaimed Hetty impetuously.

"Oh, yes!" said Rachel. "I enjoy every minute, except when the pain is too hard: you don't know what a beautiful thing life seems to me. I always have the sky you know" (glancing at the window), "and that is enough for a lifetime. Every day birds fly by too; and every day my father reads to me at least two hours. So I have great deal to think about."

"Miss Barlow, I envy you," said Hetty in a tone which startled even herself. Again Rachel bent on her the same clairvoyant gaze which had so embarrassed her before. Hetty shrank from it still more than at first, and left the room, saying to her husband: "I will wait for you outside."

As they drove away, Hetty said:

"Eben, what is it in her look which makes me so uneasy? I don't like to have her look at me."

"Now that is strange," replied the doctor. "After you had left the room, the child said to me: 'What is the matter with your wife? She is not well,' and I laughed at the idea, and told her I never knew any woman half so well or strong. Rachel is a sort of clairvoyant, as persons in her condition are so apt to be; but she made a wrong guess this time, didn't she?"

Hetty did not answer; and the doctor turning towards her saw that her eyes were fixed on the sky with a dreamy expression.

"Why, Hetty!" he exclaimed. "Why do you look so? You are perfectly well, are you not, dear?"

"Oh, yes! oh, yes!" Hetty answered, quickly rousing herself. "I am perfectly well; and always have been, ever since I can remember."

After this, Hetty went no more with her husband to see Rachel. When he asked her, she said: "No, Eben: I am going to see her alone. I will not go with you again. She makes me uncomfortable. If she makes me feel so, when I am alone with her, I shall not go at all. I don't like clairvoyants."

"Why, what a queer notion that is for you, wife!" laughed the doctor, and thought no more of it.

Hetty's first interview with Rachel was a constrained one. Nothing in Hetty's life had prepared her for intercourse with so finely organized a creature: she felt afraid to speak, lest she should wound her; her own habits of thought and subjects of interest seemed too earthy to be mentioned in this presence; she was vaguely conscious that all Rachel's being was set to finer issues than her own. She found in this an unspeakable attraction; and yet it also withheld her at every point and made her dumb. In spite of these conflicting emotions, she wanted to love Rachel, to help her, to be near her; and she went again and again, until the constraint wore off, and a very genuine affection grew up between them. Never, after the first day, had she felt any peculiar embarrassment under Rachel's gaze, and her memory of it had nearly died away, when one day, late in the autumn, it was suddenly revived with added intensity. It was a day on which Hetty had been feeling unusually sad. Even by Rachel's bedside she could not quite throw off the sadness. Unconsciously, she had been sitting for a long time silent. As she looked up, she met Rachel's eyes fixed full on hers, with the same penetrating gaze which had so disturbed her in their first interview. Rachel did not withdraw her gaze, but continued to look into Hetty's eyes, steadily, piercingly, with an expression which held Hetty spell-bound. Presently she said:

"Dear Mrs. Williams, you are thinking something which is not true. Do not let it stay with you."

"What do you mean, Rachel?" asked Hetty, resentfully. "No one can read another person's thoughts."

"Not exactly," replied Rachel, in a timid voice, "but very nearly. Since I have been ill, I have had a strange power of telling what people were thinking about: I can sometimes tell the exact words. I cannot tell how it is. I seem to read them in the air, or to hear them spoken. And I can always tell if a person is thinking either wicked thoughts or untrue ones. A wicked person always looks to me like a person in a fog. There have been some people in this room that my father thought very good; but I knew they were very bad. I could hardly see their faces clear. When a person is thinking mistaken or untrue thoughts, I see something like a shimmer of light all around them: it comes and goes, like a flicker from a candle. When you first came in to see me, you looked so."

"Pshaw, Rachel," said Hetty, resolutely. "That is all nonsense. It is just the nervous fancy of a sick girl. You mustn't give way to it."

"I should think so too," replied Rachel, meekly.

"If it did not so often come exactly true. My father will tell you how often we have tried it."

"Well, then, tell me what I was thinking just now," laughed Hetty.

Rachel colored. "I would rather not," she replied, in an earnest tone.

"Oh! you're afraid it won't prove true," said Hetty. "I'll take the risk, if you will."

Rachel hesitated, but finally repeated her first answer. "I would rather not."

Hetty persisted, and Rachel, with great reluctance, answered her as follows:

"You were thinking about yourself: you were dissatisfied about something in yourself; you are not happy, and you ought to be; you are so good."

Hetty listened with a wonder-struck face. She disliked this more than she had ever in her life disliked any thing which had happened to her. She did not speak.

"Do not be angry," said Rachel. "You made me tell you."

"Oh! I am not angry," said Hetty. "I'm not so stupid as that; but it's the most disagreeable thing, I ever knew. Can you help seeing these things, if you try?"

"Yes, I suppose I might," said Rachel. "I

never try. It interests me to see what people are thinking about."

"Humph!" said Hetty, sarcastically. "I should think so. You might make your fortune as a detective, if you were well enough to go about in the world."

"If I were that, I should lose the power," replied Rachel. "The doctors say it is part of the disease."

"Rachel," exclaimed Hetty, vehemently, "I'll never come near you again, if you don't promise not to use this power of yours upon me. I should never feel comfortable one minute where you are, if I thought you were reading my thoughts. Not that I have any special secrets," added Hetty, with a guilty consciousness; "but I suppose everybody thinks thoughts he would rather not have read."

"I'll promise you, indeed I will, dear Mrs. Williams," cried Rachel, much distressed. "I. never have read you, except that first day. It seemed forced upon me then, and to-day too. But I promise you, I will not do it again."

"I suppose I shouldn't know if you were doing it, unless you told me," said Hetty, reflectively.

"I think you would," answered Rachel. "Do I not look peculiarly? My father tells me that

"Yes, you do," replied Hetty, recollecting that, in each of these instances, she had been much disturbed by Rachel's look. "I will trust you, then, seeing that you probably can't deceive me."

When Hetty told the doctor of this, expecting that he would dismiss it as unworthy of attention, she was much surprised at the interest he showed in the account. He questioned her closely as to the expression of Rachel's face, her tones of voice, during the interval.

"And was it true, Hetty?" he asked; "was what she said true? Were you thinking of something in yourself which troubled you?"

"Yes, I was," said Hetty, in a low voice, fearing that her husband would ask her what; but he was only studying the incident from professional curiosity.

"You are sure of that, are you?" he asked.

"Yes, very sure," replied Hetty.

"Extraordinary! 'pon my word extraordinary!" ejaculated the doctor. "I have read of such cases, but I have never more than half believed them. I'd give my right hand to cure that girl."

"Your right hand is not yours to give," said Hetty, playfully. The doctor made no reply. He was deep in meditation on Rachel's clairvoyance. Hetty looked at him for some moments, as earnestly as Rachel had looked at her. "Oh if I could only have that power Rachel has!" she thought.

"Eben," she said, "is it impossible for a healthy person to be a clairvoyant?"

"Quite," answered the doctor, with a sudden instinct of what Hetty meant. "No chance for you, dear. You'll never get at any of my secrets that way. You might as well try to make yourself Rachel's age as to acquire this mysterious power she has."

Unlucky words! Hetty bore them about with her. "That showed that he feels that I am old," she said, as often as she recalled them.

A month later, as she was sitting with Rachel one morning, there was a knock at the door. Hetty was sitting in such a position that she could not be seen from the door, but could see, in the looking-glass at the foot of Rachel's bed, any person entering the room. As the door opened, she looked up, and, to her unspeakable surprise, saw her husband coming in; saw, in the same swift second's glance, the look of gladness and welcome on his face, and heard him say, in tones of great tenderness:

"How are you to-day, precious child?" In the next instant, he had seen his wife, and was, in his turn, so much astonished, that the look of glad welcome which he had bent upon Rachel, was instantaneously succeeded by one of blank surprise, bent upon Hetty; surprise, and nothing else, but so great surprise that it looked almost like dismay and confusion. "Why, Hetty!" he said, "I did not expect to see you here."

"Nor I you," said Hetty, lightly; but the lightness of tone had a certain something of constraint in it. This incident was one of those inexplicably perverse acts of Fate which make one almost believe sometimes in the depravity of spirits, if not in that of men. When Dr. Eben had left home that morning, Hetty had said to him:

"Are you going to Springton, to-day?"

"No, not to-day," was the reply.

"I am very sorry," answered Hetty. "I wanted to send some jelly to Rachel."

"Can't go to-day, possibly," the doctor had said. "I have to go the other way."

But later in the morning he had met a messenger from Springton, riding post-haste, with an imperative call which could not be deferred. And, as he was in the village, he very naturally stopped to see Rachel. All of this he explained with some confusion; feeling, for the first time in his long married life, that it was awkward for a man to have to account for his presence in any particular spot at any particular time. Hetty betrayed no annoyance or incredulity: she felt none. She was too sensible and reasonable a woman to have felt either, even if it had been simply a change of purpose on the doctor's own part which had brought him to Springton. The thing which had lent the shade of constraint to Hetty's voice, and which lay like an icy mountain on Hetty's heart, was the look which she had seen on his face, the tone which she had heard in his voice, as he greeted Rachel. In that instant was planted the second germ of unhappiness in Hetty's bosom. Of jealousy, in the ordinary acceptation of the term; of its caprices, suspicions, subterfuges; and, above all, of its resentments, — Hetty was totally incapable. If it had been made evident to her in any one moment, that her husband loved another woman, her first distinct thoughts would have been of sorrow for him rather than for herself, and of perplexity as to what could be done to make him happy again. At this moment, however, nothing took distinct shape in Hetty's mind. It was merely the vague pain of a loving woman's sensitive heart, surprised by the sight of tender looks and tones given by her husband to another woman. It was wholly a vague pain, but it was the germ of a great one; and, falling as it did on Hetty's already morbid consciousness of her own loss of youth and beauty and attractiveness, it fell into soil where such germs ripen as in a hot-bed. In a less noble nature than Hetty's there would have grown up side by side with this pain a hatred of Rachel, or, at least, an antagonism towards her. In the fine equilibrium of Hetty's moral nature, such a thing was impossible. She felt from that day a new interest in Rachel. She looked at her, often scrutinizingly, and thought: "Ah, if she were but well, what a sweet young wife she might make! I wish Eben could have had such a wife! How much better it would have been for him than having me!" She began now to go oftener with her husband to visit Rachel. Closely, but with no sinister motive, no trace of ill-feeling, she listened to all which they said. She observed the peculiar gentleness with which the doctor spoke, and the docility with which Rachel listened; and she said to herself: "That is quite unlike Eben's manner to me, or mine to him. I wonder if that is not more nearly the way it ought to be between husbands and wives. The wife ought to look up to her husband as a little child does." Now, much as Hetty loved Dr. Eben, passionately as her whole life centred around him, there had never been such a feeling as this: they were the heartiest of comrades, but each life was on a plane of absolute independence. Hetty pondered much on this.

XI.

ONE day, as they sat by Rachel's bed, the doctor had been counting her pulse. Her little white hand looked like a baby's hand in his. Holding it up, he said to Hetty:

"Look at that hand. It couldn't do much work, could it!"

Involuntarily Hetty stretched out her large, well-knit brown hand, and put it by the side of Rachel's. There are many men who would have admired Hetty's hand the more of the two. It was a much more significant hand. To one who could read palmistry, it meant all that Hetty was; and it was symmetrical and firm. But, at that moment, to Dr. Eben it looked large and masculine.

"Oh, take it away, Hetty!" he said, thoughtlessly. "It looks like a man's hand by the side of this child's."

Hetty laughed. She thought so too. But the words remained in her mind, and allied themselves to words that had gone before, and to things that had happened, and to thoughts which were restlessly growing, growing in Hetty's bosom.

If Rachel had remained an invalid, probably Hetty's thoughts of her, as connected with her husband, would never have gone beyond this vague stage which we have tried to describe. She would have been to Hetty only the suggestion of a possible ideal wife, who, had she lived, and had she entered into Dr. Eben's life, might have made him happier than Hetty could. But Rachel grew better and stronger every day. Early in the spring she began to walk, — creeping about, at first, like a little child just learning to walk, by pushing a chair before her. Then she walked with a cane and her father's arm; then with the cane alone; and at last, one day in May, — oddly enough it was the anniversary of Hetty's wedding-day, — Dr. Eben burst into her room, exclaiming: "Hetty! Hetty! Rachel has walked several rods alone. She is cured! She is going to be as well as anybody."

The doctor's face was flushed with excitement. Never had he had what seemed to him so great a professional triumph. It was the physician and not the man that felt so intensely. But

Hetty could not wholly know this. She had shared his deep anxiety about the case; and she had shared much of his strong interest in Rachel, and it was with an unaffected pleasure that she exclaimed: "Oh, I'm so thankful!" but her next sentence was one which arrested her husband's attention, and seemed to him a strange one.

"Then there is nothing to hinder her being married, is there?"

"Why, no," laughed the doctor, "nothing, except the lack of a man fit to marry her! What put such a thought as that into your head, Hetty? I don't believe Rachel Barlow will ever be married. I'm sure I don't know the man that's worthy to so much as kiss the child's feet!" and the unconscious Dr. Eben hastened away, little dreaming what a shaft he had sped.

Hetty stood at the open window, watching him, as far as she could see him, among the pines. The apple orchard, near the house, was in full bloom, and the fragrance came in at every window. A vase of the blossoms stood on Hetty's bureau: it was one of her few, tender reminiscences, the love which she had had for apple blossoms ever since the night of her marriage. She held a little cluster of them now in her hand, as she leaned on the window-sill; they had been gathered for some days, and, as a light wind stirred the air, all the petals fell, and slowly fluttered down to the ground. Hetty looked wistfully at the bare stems. A distinct purpose at that moment was forming in her mind; a purpose distinct in its aim, but, as yet, very vague in its shape. She was saying to herself: "If I were out of the way, Eben might marry Rachel. He needn't say, he doesn't know a man fit to do it. He is fit to marry any woman God ever made, and I believe he would be happier with such a wife as that, and with children, than he can ever be with me."

Even now there was in Hetty no morbid jealousy, no resentment, no suspicion that her husband had been disloyal to her even in thought. There had simply been forced upon her, by the slow accumulations of little things, the conviction that her husband would be happier with another woman for his wife than with her. It is probably impossible to portray in words all the processes of this remarkable woman's mind and heart during these extraordinary passages of her life. They will seem, judged by average standards, morbid and unhealthy: yet there was no morbidness in them; unless we are to call morbid all the great and glorious army of men and women who have laid down their own lives for the sake of others. That same fine and rare quality of self-abnegation which has inspired missionaries' lives and martyrs' deaths, inspired Hetty now. The morbidness, if there were any, was in the first entering into her mind of the belief that her husband's happiness could be secured in any way so well as by her. But here let us be just to Hetty. The view she took was the common-sense view, which probably would have been taken by nine out of ten of all Dr. Eben's friends. Who could say that it did not stand to reason, that a man would be happier with a wife, young, beautiful, of angelic sweetness of nature, and the mother of sons and daughters, than with an old, childless, and less attractive woman. The strange thing was that any wife could take this common-sense view of such a situation. It was not strange in Hetty, however. It was simply the carrying out of the impulses and motives which had characterized her whole life.

About this time, Hetty began with Raby to practise rowing on Welbury Lake. This lake was a beautiful sheet of water, lying between

Welbury and Springton. It was some two miles long, and one wide; and held two or three little wooded islands, which were much resorted to in the summer. On two sides of the lake, rose high, rocky precipices; no landing was possible there: the other two sides were thick wooded forests of pines and hemlocks. Nothing could exceed in loveliness the situation of this lake. Two roads led to it: one from the Springton, the other from the Welbury side; both running through the hemlock forests. In the winter these were used for carrying out ice, which was cut in great quantities on the lake. In the summer, no one crossed these roads, except parties of pleasure-seekers who went to sail or row on the lake. In a shanty on the Welbury side, lived an old man, who made a little money every summer by renting a few rather leaky boats, and taking charge of such boats as were kept moored at his beach by their owners.

Hetty had promised Raby that when he was ten years old he should have a fine boat, and learn to row. The time had come now for her to keep this promise. Every Saturday afternoon during the summer following Rachel's recovery, Hetty and Raby spent on the lake. Hetty was a strong and skilful oars-woman. Little

Raby soon learned to manage the boat as well as she did. The lake was considered unsafe for sail-boats, on account of flaws of wind which often, without any warning, beat down from the hills on the west side; but rowing there was one of the chief pleasures of the young people of Welbury and Springton. In Hetty's present frame of mind, this lonely lake had a strange fascination for her. In her youth she had never loved it: she had always been eager to land on one of the islands, and spend hours in the depths of the fragrant woods, rather than on the dark and silent water. But now she never wearied of rowing round and round its water margin, and looking down into its unsounded depths. It was believed that Welbury Lake was unfathomable; but this notion probably had its foundation in the limited facilities in that region for sounding deep waters.

One day Hetty rowed across the lake to the point where the Springton road came down to the shore. Pushing the boat up on the beach, she sprang out; and, telling Raby to wait there till she returned, she walked rapidly up the road. A guide-post said, "Six miles to Springton." Hetty stood some time looking reflectingly at this sign: then she walked on for half a mile, till she came to another road running north; here a guide-post said, " Fairfield, five miles." This was what Hetty was in search of. As she read the sign, she said in a low tone: " Five miles; that is easily walked." Then she turned and hastened back to the shore, stopping on the way to gather for Raby a big bunch of the snowy Indian-pipes, which grew in shining clumps in the moist dark hemlock woods. A strange and terrible idea was slowly taking possession of Hetty. Day and night it haunted her. Once having been entertained as possible, it could never be banished from her mind. How such an impulse could have become deep-seated in a nature like Hetty's will for ever remain a mystery. One would have said that she was the last woman in the world to commit a morbid or ill-regulated act. But the act she was meditating now was one which seemed like the act of insanity. Yet had Hetty never in her life seemed farther removed from any such tendency. She was calm, cheerful, self-contained. If any one saw any change in her, it seemed like nothing more than the natural increase of quiet and decorum coming with her increased age. Even her husband, when he looked back on these months, trying in anguish to remember every day, every hour, could recall no word or deed or look of hers which had seemed to him unnatural. And yet there was not a day, hardly an hour, in which her mind was not occupied with the details of a plan for going away secretly from her house, under such circumstances as to make it appear that she had been drowned in the lake. That she must leave her husband free to marry Rachel Barlow had become a fixed idea in Hetty's mind. She was too conscientious to kill herself for this purpose: moreover, she did not in the least wish to die. She was very unhappy in this keen conviction that she no longer sufficed for her husband's happiness; that she was, as she would have phrased it, "in the way." But she was not heart-broken over it, as a sentimental and feeble woman would have been. "There is plenty to do in the world," she said to herself. "I've got a good many years' work left in me yet: the thing is how to get at it." For many weeks she had revolved the matter hopelessly, till one day, as she was rowing with Raby on the lake, she heard a whistle of a steam-engine on the Springton side of the lake. In that second, her whole plan flashed upon her brain. She remembered that a railroad, leading to Canada, ran between Springton and the lake.

She remembered that there was a station not many miles from Springton. She remembered that far up in Canada was a little French village, St. Mary's, where she had once spent part of a summer with her father. St. Mary's was known far and near for its medicinal springs, and the squire had been sent there to try them. She remembered that there was a Roman Catholic priest there of whom her father had been very fond. She remembered that there were Sisters of Charity there, who used to go about nursing the sick. She remembered the physician under whose care her father was. She remembered all these things with a startling vividness in the twinkling of an eye, before the echoes of the steam-engine's whistle had died away on the air. She was almost paralyzed by the suddenness and the clearness with which she was impressed that she must go to St. Mary's. She dropped the oars, leaned forward, and looked eagerly at the opening in the woods where the Springton road touched the shore.

"What is it, aunty? What do you see!" asked Raby. The child's voice recalled her to herself.

"Nothing! nothing! Raby. I was only listening to the car-whistle. Didn't you hear it?" answered Hetty.

"No," said Raby. "Where are they going? Can't you take me some day."

The innocent words smote on Hetty's heart. How should she leave Raby? What would her life be without him? his without her? But thinking about herself had never been Hetty's habit. That a thing would be hard for her had never been to Hetty any reason for not doing it, since she was twelve years old. From all the pain and loss which were involved to her in this terrible step she turned resolutely away, and never thought about them except with a guilty sense of selfishness. She believed with all the intensity of a religious conviction that it would be better for her husband, now, to have Rachel Barlow for his wife. She believed, with the same intensity, that she alone stood in the way of this good for him. Call it morbid, call it unnatural, call it wicked if you will, in Hetty Williams to have this belief: you must judge her conduct from its standpoint, and from no other. The belief had gained possession of her. She could no more gainsay it, resist it, than if it had been communicated to her by supernatural beings of visible presence and actual speech. Given this belief, then her whole conduct is lifted to a plane of heroism, takes rank with the grand martyrdoms; and is not to be lightly condemned by any who remember the words, — "Greater love hath no man than this, that a man lay down his life for his friend."

The more Hetty thought over her plan, the simpler and more feasible it appeared. More and more she concentrated all her energies on the perfecting of every detail: she left nothing unthought of, either in her arrangements for her own future, or in her arrangements for those she left behind. Her will had been made for many years, leaving unreservedly to her husband the whole estate of "Gunn's," and also all her other property, except a legacy to Jim and Sally, and a few thousand dollars to old Cæsar and Nan. Hetty was singularly alone in the world. She had no kindred to whom she felt that she owed a legacy. As she looked forward to her own departure, she thought with great satisfaction of the wealth which would now be her husband's. "He will sell the farm, no doubt, — it isn't likely that he will care to live on here; and when he has it all in money he can go to Europe, as he has so often said he would," she said to herself, still, as ever, planning for her husband's enjoyment.

As the autumn drew near, she went oftener

with Raby to row on the Lake. A spell seemed to draw her to the spot. She continually lived over, in her mind, all the steps she must take when the time came. She rowed slowly back and forth past the opening of the Springton road, and fancied her own figure walking alone up that bank for the last time. Several times she left Raby in the boat, and walked as far as the Fairfield guide-post, and returned. At last she had rehearsed the terrible drama so many times that it almost seemed to her as if it had already happened, and she found it strange to be in her own house with her husband and Jim and Sally and her servants. Already she began to feel herself dissevered from them. When every thing was ready, she shrank from taking the final step. Three times she went with Raby to the Lake, having determined within herself not to return; but her courage failed her, and she found a ready excuse for deferring all until the next day. She had forgotten some little thing, or the weather looked threatening; and the last time she went back, it was simply to kiss her husband again. "One day more or less cannot make any difference," she said to herself. "I will kiss Eben once more." Oh, what a terrible thing is this barrier of flesh, which separates soul from soul, even in the closest relation! Our nearest and dearest friend, sitting so near that we can hear his every breath, can see if his blood runs by a single pulse-beat faster to his cheek, may yet be thinking thoughts which, if we could read them, would break our hearts. When the time came in which Eben Williams tried to recall the last moments in which he had seen his wife, all he could recollect was that she kissed him several times with more than usual affection. At the time he had hardly noted it: he was just setting off to see a patient, and Raby was urging Hetty to make haste; and their good-byes had been hurried.

It was on a warm hazy day in October. The woods through which Hetty and Raby walked to the lake were full of low dogwood bushes, whose leaves were brilliant; red, pink, yellow, and in places almost white. Raby gathered boughs of these, and carried them to the boat. It was his delight to scatter such bright leaves from the stern of the boat, and watch them following in its wake. They landed on the small island nearest the Springton shore, and looked for wild grapes, which were now beginning to be ripe. After an hour or two here, Hetty told Raby that they must set out: she had errands to do in the town before going home. She rowed very quickly to the beach, and, just as they were leaving the boat, she exclaimed:

"Oh, Raby, I have left my shawl on the island; way around on the other side it is too. I must row back and get it."

Raby was about to jump into the boat, but she exclaimed:

"No, you stay here, and wait. I can row a great deal quicker with only one in the boat. Here, dear," she said, taking off her watch, and hanging it round his neck, "you can have this to keep you from being lonely, and you can tell by this how long it will be before I get back. Watch the hands, and that will make the time seem shorter, they go so fast. It will take me about half an hour; that will be — let me see — yes — just five o'clock. There is a good long daylight after that;" and, kissing him, she jumped into the boat and pushed off. What a moment it was. Her arms seemed to be paralyzed; but, summoning all her will, she drove the boat resolutely forward, and looked no more back at Raby. As soon as she had gained the other side of the island, where she was concealed from Raby's sight by the trees, she pulled out vigorously for the Springton shore. When she reached it, she drew the boat up cautiously on the beach, fastened it, and hid herself among the trees. Her plan was to wait there until dusk, then push the boat adrift in the lake, and go out herself adrift into the world. She dared not set out on her walk to Fairfield until it was dark; she knew, moreover, that the northern train did not pass until nearly midnight. These hours that Hetty spent crouched under the hemlock-trees on the shore of the lake were harder than any which she lived through afterward. She kept her eyes fixed on the opposite shore, on the spot where she knew the patient child was waiting for her. She pictured him walking back and forth, trying by childish devices to while away the time. As the sun sank low she imagined his first anxious look, — his alarm, — till it seemed impossible for her to bear the thoughts her imagination called up. He would wait, she thought, about one hour past the time that she had set for her return: possibly, for he was a brave child, he might wait until it began to grow dark; he would think that she was searching for the shawl. She hoped that any other explanation of her absence would not occur to him until the very last. As the twilight deepened into dusk, the mysterious night sounds began to come up from the woods; strange bird notes, stealthy steps of tiny creatures. Hetty's nerves thrilled with the awful loneliness: she could bear it no longer; she began to walk up and down the beach; the sound of her footsteps drowned many of the mysterious noises, and made her feel less alone. At last it was dark. With all her strength she turned her boat bottom side up, shoved it out into the lake, and threw the oars after it. Then she wrapped herself in a dark cloak, and walked at a rapid pace up the Springton road. When she reached the road which led to Fairfield, she stopped, leaned against the guide-post, and looked back and hesitated. It seemed as if the turning northward were the turning point of every thing. Her heart was very heavy: almost her purpose failed her. "It is too late to go back now," she said, and hurried on.

XII.

THE station-master at Fairfield, if he had been asked whether a woman took the midnight train north at Fairfield that night, would have unhesitatingly said, " No." An instinctive wisdom seemed to direct Hetty's every step. She waited at some little distance from the station till the train came up : then, without going upon the station platform at all, she entered the rear car from the opposite side of the road. No one saw her ; not even a brakeman. When the train began to move, the sense of what she had done smote her with a sudden terror, and she sprang to her feet, but sank down again, before any of the sleepy passengers had observed her motion. In a few moments she was calm. Her long habits of firm, energetic action began to resume sway : she compelled herself to look forward into the future, and not backward into the past she was so resolutely leaving behind her. Strangely enough, it was not her husband that she found hardest to banish from her thoughts now, but Raby. She could not escape from the vivid imagination of the dear child running in terror alone through the long stretch of woods.

"I wonder if he will cry," thought poor Hetty: "I hope not." And the tears filled her eyes. Then she fell to wondering if there would be any doubt in anybody's mind that her boat had suddenly capsized. "They will think I leaned over to pick something off the bushes on the edge of the island," said she. "I have come very near capsizing that way more than once, and I have always told Eben when it had happened. That is the first thing he will think of." And thus, in a maze of incoherent crowding conjectures and imaginings, all making up one great misery, Hetty sat whirling away from her home. By and by, her brain grew less active; thought was paralyzed by pain. She sat motionless, taking no note of the hours of the night as they sped by, and roused from her dull reverie only when she saw the first faint red tinge of dawn in the eastern sky. Then she started up, with a fresh realization of all. "Oh, it is morning!" she said. "Have they given over looking for me, I wonder. I suppose they have been looking all night. By this time, they must be sure I am drowned. After I know all that is over, I shall feel easier. It can't be quite so hard to bear as this."

In all Hetty's imaginings of her plan, she had leaped over the interval of transition from the life she left to the life she proposed to lead. She had pictured herself always as having attained the calm rest of the shelter she would seek, the strong moral support of the work she would do. She had not dwelt on this wretched interval of concealment and flight; she had not thought of this period of being an unknown outcast. A sense of ignominy began to crush her. It was a new thing for her to avoid a human eye: she felt guilty, ashamed, terror-stricken; and, doubly veiling her face, she sat with her eyes closed, and her head turned away, like one asleep or ill. The day dragged slowly on. Now and then she left the train, and bought a new ticket to carry her farther. Even had there been suspicions of her flight, it would have been impossible to have traced her, so skilfully had she managed. She had provided herself with a time-table of the entire route, and bought new tickets only at points of junction where several roads met, and no attention could possibly be drawn to any one traveller.

At night she reached the city, where she had planned to remain for some days, to make purchases. When she entered the hotel, and was asked to register her name, no one who saw the quick and ready signature which she wrote would have dreamed that it was not her own:

"Mrs. HIBBA SMAILLI,
St. Mary's,
Canada."

"One of those Welsh women, from St. Mary's, I guess," said the clerk; "they all have those fresh, florid skins when they first come over here." And with this remark he dismissed Hetty from his mind, only wondering now and then, as he saw her so often coming in, laden with parcels, "what a St. Mary's woman wanted with so many things."

During these days, while Hetty was unflinchingly going forward with all her preparations for her new home, the home she had left was a scene of terrible dismay and suffering.

It was long after dark when little Raby, breathless and sobbing, had burst open the sitting-room door, crying out:

"Auntie's drowned in the lake. I know she is; or else a bear's eaten her up. She said she'd be back in an hour. And here's her watch," — opening his little hot hand, in which he had held the watch tight through all his running, — "she gave it to me to hold till she came back. And she said it would be five; and I stayed till seven, and she never came; and a man brought me home." And Raby flung himself on the floor, crying convulsively.

His father and mother tried to calm him, and to get a more exact account from him of what had happened; but, between their alarm and his hysterical crying, all was confusion.

Presently, the man entered who had brought Raby home in his wagon. He was a stranger to them all. His narrative merely corroborated Raby's, but threw no light on what had gone before. He had found the child on the main road, running very fast, and crying aloud. He had asked him to jump into his wagon; and Raby had replied: "Yes, sir: if you will whip your horse and make him run all the way to my house? My auntie's drowned in the lake;" and this was all the child had said.

Poor Raby! his young nerves had entirely given way under the strain of those hours of anxious waiting. He had borne the first hour very well. When the watch said it was five o'clock, and Hetty was not in sight, he thought, as she had hoped he would, that she was searching for the shawl; but, when six o'clock came, and her boat was not in sight, his childish heart took alarm. He ran to the shanty where the old boatman lived; and pounded furiously on the door, shouting loud, for the man was very deaf. The door was locked; no one answered. Raby pushed logs under the windows, and, climbing up, looked in. The house was empty. Then the little fellow jumped into the only boat which was there, and began to row out into the lake in search of Hetty.

Alas! the boat leaked so fast that it was with difficulty he got back to the shore. Perhaps, if Hetty, from her hiding-place, had seen the dear, brave child rowing to her rescue, it might have been a rescue indeed. It might have changed for ever the current of her life. But this was not to be. Wet and chilled, and clogged by his dripping shoes, Raby turned towards home. The woods were dark and full of shadows. The child had never been alone in them at night before; and the gloom added to his terrors. His feet seemed as if they would fail him at every step, and his sobbing cries left him little breath with which to run.

Jim and Sally turned helplessly to the stranger, as he concluded his story.

"Oh, what shall we do! what shall we do!" they said. "Oh, take us right back to the lake, won't you? and the rest will follow: we may find her."

"There isn't any boat," cried Raby, from the floor. "I tried to go for her, and the boat is all full of holes, and she must have been drowned ever so long by this time; she told me it only took half an hour, that nobody could be brought to life after that," and Raby's cries rose almost to shrieks, and brought old Cæsar and Nan from the kitchen. As the first words of what had happened reached their ears, they broke into piercing lamentations. Nan, with inarticulate groans, and Cæsar with, "Damn! damn! bress de Lord! No, damn! damn! dat lake. Haven't I always told Miss Hetty not to be goin' there. Oh, damn! damn! no, no, bress de Lord!" and the old man, clasping both hands above his head, rushed to the barn to put the horses into the big farm-wagon. With anguished hearts, and hopelessly, Jim and Sally piled blankets and pillows into the wagon, and took all the restoratives they could think of. They knew in their hearts all would be of no use. As they drove through the village they gave the alarm; and, in an incredibly short time, the whole shore of the lake was twinkling with lights borne high in the hands of men who were searching. Two boats were rowing back and forth on the lake, with bright lights at stern and prow; and loud shouts filled the air. No answer; no clew: at last, from the island, came a pistol shot,—the signal agreed on. Every man stood still and listened. Slowly the boats came back to shore, drawing behind them Hetty's boat; bringing one of the oars, and also Hetty's shawl, which they had found, just where Raby had told them they would, in the wild-grape thicket.

"Found it bottom-side up," was all that the men said, as they shoved the boat high up on the sand. Then they all looked in each other's faces, and said no more. There was nothing more to be done: it was now ten o'clock. Slowly the sad procession wound back to town through the rayless hemlock woods. Midway in them, they met a rider, riding at the maddest gallop. It was the doctor! No one had known where to send for him; and there was no time to be lost. Coming home, and wondering, as he entered, at the open doors and the unlighted windows, he had found Norah sitting on the floor by the weeping Raby, and trying to comfort him. Barely comprehending, in his sudden distress what they told him, the doctor had sprung upon his horse and galloped towards the lake. As he saw the group of people moving towards him, looking shadowy and dim in the darkness, his heart stood still. Were they bearing home Hetty's body? Would he see it presently, lying lifeless and cold in their arms? He dashed among them, reining his horse back on his haunches, and looking with a silent anguish into face after face. Nobody spoke. That first instant seemed a century long. Nobody could speak. At a glance the doctor saw that they were not bearing the sad burden he had feared.

"Not found her?" he gasped.

"No, doctor," replied one nearest him, laying his hand on his arm.

"Then by God what have you come away for! have you got the souls of men in you?" exclaimed Eben Williams, in a voice which seemed to shake the very trees, as he plunged onward.

"It's no use, doctor," they replied sadly.

"We found her boat bottom up, and one of the oars; and it was hours since it capsized."

"What then!" he shouted back. "My wife was as strong as any man: she can't have drowned; Hetty can't have drowned;" and his horse's hoofs struck sparks from the stones as he galloped on. A few of the younger men turned back and followed him; but, when they reached the lake, he was nowhere to be seen. Old Cæsar, who was sitting on the ground, his head buried on his knees, said:

"He wouldn't hear a word. He jest jumped into one of thim boats, and he was gone like lightning: he's 'way across the lake by this time."

Silently the young men re-entered their boats and rowed out, carrying torches. Presently they overtook the doctor.

"Oh, thank God for that light!" he exclaimed, "Give one to me; let me have it here in my boat: I shall find her."

Like a being of superhuman strength, the doctor rowed; no one could keep up with him. Round and round the lake, into every inlet, close under the shadows of the islands; again and again, over every mile of that treacherous, glassy, beautiful water, he rowed, calling every few moments, in heart-breaking tones, "Hetty! Hetty! Hetty! I am here, Hetty!"

As the hours wore on, his strength began to flag; he rowed more and more slowly: but, when they begged him to give over the search, and return home, he replied impatiently. "Never! I'll never leave this lake till I find her." It was useless to reason with him. He hardly heard the words. At last, his friends, worn out by the long strain, rowed to the shore, and left him alone. As he bade them good-by, he groaned, "Oh, God! will it never be morning? If only it were light, I am sure I should find some trace of her." But, when the morning broke, the pitiless lake shone clear and still, and all the hopelessness of his search flashed on the bereaved man's mind: he dropped his oars, and gazed vacantly over the rippleless surface. Then he buried his face in his hands, and sat motionless for a long time: he was trying to recall Hetty's last looks, last words. He recollected her last kisses. "It was as if they were to bid me good-bye," he thought. Presently, he took up the oars and rowed back to the shore. Old Cæsar still sat there on the ground. The doctor touched him on the shoulder. He lifted a face so wan, so altered, that the doctor started.

"My poor old fellow," he said, "you ought not to have sat here all night. We will go home now. There is nothing more to be done."

"Oh, yer ain't a goin' to give up, doctor, be

yer?" cried Cæsar. "Oh, don't never give up. She must be here somewheres. Bodies floats allers in fresh water: she 'll come to shore before long. Oh, don't give up! I 'll set here an' watch, an' you go home an' git somethin' to eat. You looks dreadful."

"No, no, Cæsar," the doctor replied, with the first tears he had felt yet welling up in his eyes, "you must come home with me. There is no hope of finding her."

Cæsar did not move, but fixed a sullen gaze on the water. The doctor spoke again, more firmly:

"You must come, Cæsar. Your mistress would tell you so herself." At this Cæsar rose, docile, and the two went home in silence through the hemlock woods.

For three days the search for Hetty continued. It was suggested that possibly she might have gone over to the Springton shore for some purpose, and there have met with some accident or assault. This suggestion opened up new vistas of conjecture, almost more terrible than the certainty of her death would have been. Parties of three and four scoured the woods in all directions. Again and again Dr. Eben passed over the spot where she had lain crouched so long : the bushes which had been brushed back as she passed, bent back again to let him go over her very footsteps ; but nothing could speak to betray her secret. Nature seems most mute when we most need her help: she keeps, through all our distresses, a sort of dumb and faithful neutrality, which is not, perhaps, so devoid of sympathy as it appears.

After the third day was over, it was accepted by tacit consent that farther search would be useless. Hetty was mourned as dead: in every home her name was tenderly and sorrowingly spoken ; old memories of her gay and mirthful youth, of her cheery and busy womanhood, were revived and dwelt upon. But in her own home was silence that could be felt. The grief there was grief that could not speak. Only little Raby, of all the household, found words to use ; and his childish and inconsolable laments made the speechless anguish around him all the greater. To Dr. Eben, the very sight of the child was a bitter and unreasonable pain. Except for Raby, he thought, Hetty would still be alive. He had never approved of her taking him on the water ; had remonstrated with her in the beginning, but had been overruled by her impetuous confidence in her own strength and skill. Now, as often as he saw the poor little fellow's woe-begone face, he had a strange mixture of pity and hatred towards him. In vain he reasoned against it. "He has lost his best friend, as well as I," he said to himself; "I ought to try to comfort him." But it was impossible: the child's presence grew more and more irksome to him, until, at last, he said to Sally, one day:

"Sally, you and Raby are both looking very ill. I want you to go away for a time. How would you like to go to 'The Runs,' for a month?"

"Oh, not there, dear doctor! please do not send us there!" cried Sally. "Indeed I could not bear it. We might go to father's for a while. That would be change enough; and Raby would have children to play with there, in the village, all the time, and that would be the best thing for him."

So Jim and Sally went to Deacon Little's to stay for a time. Mrs. Little welcomed them with a cordiality which it would have done Hetty's heart good to see. Her old aversion to Sally had been so thoroughly conquered that she was more than half persuaded in her own mind it had never existed. When the doctor was left alone in the house, he found it easier to bear the burden of his grief. It is only after the first shock of a great sorrow is past that we are helped by faces and voices and the clasping of hands. At the first, there is but one help, but one healing; and that is solitude.

Dr. Eben came out from this grief an altered man. Poor Hetty! How little she had understood her value to her husband! Could she have seen him walking slowly from house to house, his eyes fixed on the ground, his head bent forward; all his old elasticity of tread gone; his ready smile gone; the light, glad look of his eyes gone, — how would she have repented her rash and cruel deed! how would the scales have fallen from her eyes, revealing to her the monstrous misapprehension to which she had sacrificed her life and his! Even long after people had ceased to talk about Hetty's death, or to remember it unless they saw the doctor, the first sight of his tall bowed figure recalled it all; and again and again, as he passed men on the street, they turned and said to each other, with a sad shake of the head:

"He's never got over it."

"No, nor ever will."

On the surface, life seemed to be going on at "Gunn's" much as before. Jim and Sally and

Raby made a family centre, to which the lonely doctor attached himself more and more. He came more and more to feel that Raby was a legacy left by Hetty to him. He had ceased to have any unjust resentment towards the child from his innocent association with her death: he knew that she had loved the boy as if he were her own; and, in his long sad reveries about the future, he found a sort of melancholy pleasure in planning for Raby as he would have done had he been Hetty's child. These plans for Raby, and his own devotion to his profession, were Dr. Eben's only pleasure. He was fast becoming a physician of note. He was frequently sent for in consultation to all parts of the county; and his contributions to medical journals were held in high esteem. The physician, the student, had gained unspeakably by the loss which had so nearly crushed the man.

Development and strength, gained at such cost, are like harvests springing out of land which had to be burned black with fire before it would yield its increase.

XIII.

HETTY first entered the village of St. Mary's at sunset. The chapel bell was ringing for the Angelus, and as the nondescipt little vehicle, half diligence half coach, crept through the sandy streets, Hetty, looking eagerly out, saw men, women, and children falling on their knees by the road-side. She recollected having noted this custom when she was in St. Mary's before: then it had seemed to her senseless mummery; now it seemed beautiful. Hetty had just come through dark places, in which she had wanted help from God more than she had ever in her life wanted it; and these evident signs of faith, of an established relation between earth and heaven, fell most gratefully upon her aching heart. The village of St. Mary's is a mere handful of houses, on a narrow stretch of sandy plain, lying between two forests of firs. Many years ago, hunters, finding in the depths of these forests springs of great medicinal value, made a little clearing about them, and built there a few rough shanties to which they might at any time resort for the waters. Gradually, the fame of the waters was noised abroad, and drew settlers to the spot. The clearing was widened; houses were built; a village grew up; line after line, as a new street was needed, the forests were cut down, but remained still a solid, dark-green wall and background to the east and the west. On the outskirts of the village, in the edge of the western forest, stood the Roman Catholic chapel, — a low wooden building, painted red, and having a huge silver cross on the top.

At the moment of Hetty's arrival, a burial service was just about to take place in this little chapel, and the procession was slowly approaching: the priest walking in front, lifting up a high gilt crucifix; a little white-robed acolyte carrying holy water in a silver basin; a few Sisters of Charity with their long black gowns and flapping white bonnets; behind these the weeping villagers, bearing the coffin on a rude sort of litter. As Hetty saw this procession, she was seized with an irresistible desire to join it. She was the only passenger in the diligence, and the door was locked. She called to the driver, and at last succeeded in making him hear, and also understand that she wished to be set down immediately: she would walk on to the inn. She wished first to go into the church. The driver was a good Catholic; very seriously he said: "It is bad luck to say one's prayers while there is going on the mass for the dead; there is another chapel which Madame would find less sad at this hour. It is only a short distance farther on."

But Hetty reiterated her request; and the driver, shrugging his shoulders, and saying in an altered tone:

"As Madame pleases; it is all the same to me: nevertheless, it is bad luck;" assisted her to alight.

The procession had just entered the church. Dim lights twinkled on the altar, and a smell of incense filled the place. Hetty fell on her knees with the rest, and prayed for those she had left behind her. Her prayer was simple and short, repeated many times: "Oh God, make them happy! make them happy!" When the mass was over, Hetty waited near the door, and watched anxiously to see if the priest were the same whom her father had known so well twenty years before. Yes, it was — no — could this be Father Antoine? This fat, red-faced, jovial-looking old man? Father Antoine had been young, slender and fair; but there was no mistaking the calm and serious hazel eyes. It was Father Antoine, but how changed!

"If I have changed as much as that," thought Hetty, "he'll never believe I am I; and I dare say I have. Dear me, what a frightful thing is this old age!"

Hetty had resolved, in the outset, that she would take Father Antoine into her confidence. She knew the sacredness of secrecy in which Roman Catholic priests are accustomed to hold all confessions made to them. She felt that her secret would be too heavy to bear unshared, and that times might arise when she would need advice or help from one knowing all the truth.

Early the next morning, she went to Father Antoine's house. The good old man was at work in his garden. His little cottage was surrounded by beds which were gay with flowers from June till November. Nothing was left in bloom now, except asters and chrysanthemums: but there was no flower, not even his July carnations, in which he took such pride, as in his chrysanthemums. As he heard the little gate shut, he looked up; saw that it was a stranger; and came forward to meet her, bearing in his hand one great wine-colored chrysanthemum blossom, as large as a blush rose:

"Is it to see me, daughter?" he said, with his inalienable old French courtesy. Father Antoine had come of a race which had noble blood in its veins. His ancestry had worn swords, and lived at courts, and Antoine Ladeau never once, in his half century of work in these Canadian forests, forgot that fact. Hetty looked him full in the face, and colored scarlet, before she began to speak.

"You do not remember me," she said.

Father Antoine shook his head. "It is that I see so many faces each year," he replied apologetically, "that it is not possible to remember;" and he gazed earnestly into Hetty's expressive face.

"It is twenty years since I was here," Hetty continued. She felt a great longing that Father Antoine should recollect her. It would seem to make her task easier.

A reminiscence dawned on the priest's mind. "Twenty years?" he said, "ah, but that is long! we were both young then. Is it — ah, is it possible that it is the daughter with the father that I see?" Father Antoine had never forgotten the beautiful relation between Hetty and her father.

"Yes, I came with my father: you knew him very well," replied Hetty, "and I always thought then that, if I had any trouble, I would like to have you help me."

Father Antoine's merry face clouded over instantly. "And have you trouble, my daughter? If the good God permits that I help you, I shall be glad. I had a love for your father. He is no longer alive, or you would not be in trouble;" and, leading Hetty into his little study, Father Antoine sat down opposite her, and said:

"Tell me, my daughter."

Hetty's voice trembled, and tears filled her eyes: sympathy was harder to bear than loneliness. The story was hard to tell, but she told it, without pause, without reserve. Father Antoine's face grew stern as she proceeded. When she ceased speaking, he said:

"My daughter, you have sinned; sinned grievously: you must return to your husband. You have violated a holy sacrament of the Church. I command you to return to your husband."

Hetty stared at him in undisguised wonder. At last she said:

"Why do you speak to me like that, sir? I can obey no man: only my own conscience is my law. I will never return to my husband."

"The Church is the conscience of all her erring children," replied Father Antoine, "and disobedience is at the peril of one's soul. I lay it upon you, as the command of the Church, that you return, my daughter. You have sinned most grievously."

"Oh," said Hetty, with apparent irrelevance. "I understand now. You took me for a Catholic."

It was Father Antoine's turn to stare.

"Why then, if you are not, came you to me?" he said sternly. "I am here only as priest."

Hetty clasped her hands, and said pleadingly:

"Oh no! not only as priest: you are a good man. My father always said so. We were not Catholics; and I could not be of any other religion than my father's, now he is dead," (here Hetty unconsciously touched a chord in Antoine Ladeau's breast, which gave quick response): "but I recollected how he trusted you, and I said, if I can hide myself in that little village, Father Antoine will be good to me for my father's sake. But you must not tell me to go back to my home: no one can judge about that but me. The thing I have done is best: I shall not go back. And, if you will not keep my secret and be my friend, I will go away at once and hide myself in some other place still farther away, and will ask no one again to be my friend, ever till I die!"

Father Antoine was perplexed. All the blood of ancient knighthood which was in his veins was stirred with chivalrous desire to help Hetty: but, on the other hand, both as man and as priest, he felt that she had committed a great wrong, and that he could not even appear to countenance it. He studied Hetty's face: in spite of its evident marks of pain, it was as indomitable as rock.

"You have the old Huguenot soul, my daughter," he said. "Antoine Ladeau knows better than to try to cause you to swerve from the path you have chosen. But the good God can give you light: it may be that he has directed you here to find it in his true Church. Be sure that your father was a good Catholic at heart."

"Oh, no! he wasn't," exclaimed Hetty, impetuously. "There was nothing he disliked so much as a Catholic. He always said you were the only Catholic he ever saw that he could trust."

Father Antoine's rosy face turned rosier. He was not used among his docile Canadians to any such speech as this. The unvarnished fashions of New England honesty grated on his ear.

"It is not well for men of one religion to rail at the men of another," he said gravely. "I doubt not, there are those whom the Lord loves in all religions; but there is but one true Church."

"Forgive me," said Hetty, in a meeker tone. "I did not mean to be rude: but I thought I ought not to let you have such a mistaken idea about father. Oh, please, be my friend, Father Antoine!"

Father Antoine was silent for a time. Never had he been so sorely perplexed. The priest and the man were arrayed against each other.

Presently he said:

"What is it that you would have me do, my daughter? I do not see that there is any thing; since you have so firm a will and acknowledge not the Church."

"Oh!" said Hetty, perceiving that he relented, "there is not any thing that I want you to do, exactly. I only want to feel that there is one person who knows all about me, and will keep my secret, and is willing to be my friend. I shall not want any help about any thing, unless it is to get work; but I suppose they always want nurses here. There will be plenty to do."

"Daughter, I will keep your secret," said Father Antoine, solemnly: "about that you need have had no fear. No man of my race has ever betrayed a trust; and I will be your friend, if you need aught that I can do, while you choose to live in this place. But I shall pray daily to the good God to open your eyes, and make you see that you are living in heinous sin each day that you live away from your husband;" and Father Antoine rose with the involuntary habit of the priest of dismissing a parishioner when there was no more needful to be said. Hetty took her leave with a feeling of meek gratitude, hitherto unknown in her bosom. Spite of Father Antoine's disapproval, spite of his arbitrary Romanism, she trusted and liked him.

"It is no matter if he does think me wrong," she said to herself. "That needn't disturb me if I know I am right. I think he is wrong to pray to the Virgin and the saints."

Hetty had brought with her a sum of money more than sufficient to buy a little cottage, and fit it up with all needful comforts. She had no sentimental dispositions towards deprivation and wretchedness. All her plannings looked toward a useful, cheery, comfortable life. Among her purchases were gardening utensils, which she could use herself, and seeds and shrubs suited to the soil of St. Mary's. Strangely enough, the only cottage which she could find at all adapted to her purpose was one very near Father Antoine's, and almost precisely like it. It stood in the edge of the forest, and had still left in its enclosure many of the stumps of recently felled trees. All Hetty's farmer's instincts revived in full force; and, only a few days after Father Antoine's conversation with her, he found her one morning superintending the uprooting of these stumps, and making preparations for grading the land. As he watched her active movements, energetic tones, and fresh open face, he fell into a maze of wondering thought. This was no morbid sentimentalist; no pining, heart-broken woman. Except that truthfulness was stamped on every lineament of Hetty's countenance, Father Antoine would have doubted her story; and, except that her every act showed such vigorous common sense, he would have doubted her sanity. As it was, his perplexity deepened; so also did his interest in her. It was impossible not to admire this brisk, kindly, outspoken woman, who already moved about in the village with a certain air of motherly interest in every thing and everybody; had already begun to "help" in her own sturdy fashion, and had already won the goodwill of old and young.

"The good God will surely open her eyes in his own time," thought Father Antoine, and in his heart he pondered much what a good thing it would be, if, when that time came, Hetty could be persuaded to become the Lady Superior of the Convent of the Bleeding Heart, only a few miles from St. Mary's. "She is born for an abbess," he said to himself: "her will is like the will of a man, but she is full of succor and tender offices. She would be a second Angélique, in her fervor and zeal." And the good old priest said rosaries full of prayers for Hetty, night and day.

There were two "Houses of Cure" in St. Mary's, both under the care of skilful physicians, who made specialties of treatment with the waters of the springs. One of these physicians was a Roman Catholic, and employed no nurses except the Sisters from the Convent of the Bleeding Heart. They came in turn, in bands of six or eight; and stayed three months at a time. In the other House, under the care of an English physician, nurses were hired without reference to their religion. As soon as Hetty's house was all in order, and her shrubs and trees set out, she went one morning to this House, and asked to see the physician in charge. With characteristic brevity, she stated that she had come to St.

Mary's to earn her living as a nurse, and would like to secure a situation. The doctor looked at her scrutinizingly.

"Have you ever nursed?"

"No, sir."

"What do you know about it then?"

"I have seen a great many sick people."

"How was that?"

Hetty hesitated, but with some confusion replied:

"My husband was a doctor, and I often went with him to see his patients."

"You are a widow then?"

"No, sir."

"What then?" said the physician, severely.

Poor Hetty! She rose to her feet; but, recollecting that she had no right to be indignant, sat down, and replied in a trembling voice:

"I cannot tell you, sir, any thing about my trouble. I have come here to live, and I want to be a nurse."

"Father Antoine knows me," she added, with dignity.

Father Antoine's name was a passport. Doctor Macgowan had often wished that he could have all his nurses from the convent.

"You are a Catholic, then?" he said.

"No, indeed!" exclaimed Hetty, emphatically. "I am nothing of the sort."

"How is it that you mention Father Antoine, then?"

"He knew my father well, and me also, years ago; and he is the only friend I have here."

Dr. Macgowan had an Englishman's instinctive dislike of unexplained things and mysterious people. But Hetty's face and voice were better than pedigrees and certificates. Her confident reference to Father Antoine was also enough to allay any immediate uneasiness, and, "for the rest, time will show," thought the doctor; and, without any farther delay, he engaged Hetty as one of the day nurses in his establishment. In after years Dr. Macgowan often looked back to this morning, and thought, with the sort of shudder with which one looks back on a danger barely escaped:

"Good God! what if I had let that woman go?"

All Hetty's native traits especially adapted her to the profession of nursing; and her superb physical health was of itself a blessing to every sick man or sick woman with whom she came in contact. Before she had been in Dr. Macgowan's house one week, all the patients had learned to listen in the morning for her step and her voice: they all wanted her, and begged to be put under her charge.

"Really, Mrs. Smailli, I shall have to cut you up into parcels," said the doctor one day: "there is not enough of you to go round. You have a marvellous knack at making sick people like you. Did you really never nurse before?"

"Not with my hands and feet," replied Hetty, "but I think I have always been a nurse at heart. I have always been so well that to be sick seems to me the most dreadful thing in the world. I believe it is the only trouble I couldn't bear."

"You do not look as if you had ever had any very hard trouble of any kind," said the doctor in a light tone, but watching keenly the effect of his words.

Dr. Macgowan was beginning to be tormented by a great desire to know more in regard to his new nurse. Father Antoine's guarded replies to all his inquiries about her had only stimulated his curiosity.

"She is a good woman. You may trust her with all your house," Father Antoine had said; and had told the doctor that he had known both her and her father twenty years ago. More than this he would not say, farther than to express the opinion that she would live and die in St. Mary's, and devote herself to her work so long as she lived.

"She has for it a grand vocation, as we say."

Father Antoine exclaimed, "A grand vocation! Ah! if we but had her in our convent!"

"You'll never get her there as long as I'm alive, Father Antoine!" Dr. Macgowan had replied. "You may count upon that."

When Dr. Macgowan said to Hetty:

"You do not look as if you had ever had any very hard trouble of any kind," Hetty looked in his face eagerly, and answered:

"Do I not, really? I am so thankful, doctor! I have always had such a dread of looking woe-begone, and making everybody around me uncomfortable. I think that's a sin, if one can possibly help it."

And by no sudden surprise of remark or question, could the doctor ever come any nearer to Hetty's trouble than this. Her words always glanced off from direct personal issues, as subtlely and successfully as if she had been a practised diplomatist. Sometimes these perpetual evadings and non-committals seemed to Dr. Macgowan like art; but they were really the very simplicity of absolute unselfishness; and, gradually, as he came to perceive and understand this, he came to have a reverence for Hetty. He began to be ashamed of the curiosity he had felt as to the details of the sorrow which had driven her to this refuge of isolation and hard work. He began to feel about her as Father Antoine did, that there was a certain sacredness in her vocation which almost demanded a recognition of title, an investiture of office. Hetty would have been astonished, and would have very likely laughed, had she known with what a halo of sentiment her daily life was fast being surrounded in the minds of people. To her it was simply a routine of good, wholesome work; of a kind for which she was best fitted, and which enabled her to earn a comfortable living most easily to herself, and most helpfully to others; and left her "less time to think," as she often said to herself, "than any thing else I could possibly have done." "Time to think" was the one thing Hetty dreaded. As resolutely as if they were a sin, she strove to keep out of her mind all reminiscences of her home, all thoughts of her husband, of Raby. Whenever she gave way to them, she was unfitted for work; and, therefore, her conscience said they were wrong. While she was face to face with suffering ones, and her hands were busy in ministering to their wants, such thoughts never intruded upon her. It was literally true that, in such hours, she never recollected that she was any other than Hibba Smailli, the nurse. But, when her day's work was done, and she went home to the little lonely cottage, memories flocked in at the silent door, shut themselves in with her, and refused to be banished. Hence she formed the habit of lingering in the street, of chatting with the villagers on their door-steps, playing with the children, and often, when there was illness in any of the houses, going into them, and volunteering her services as nurse.

The St. Mary's people were, almost without exception, of French descent, and still kept up many of the old French customs of out-door *fêtes* and ceremonies. Hetty found their joyous, child-like ways and manners singularly attractive and interesting. After the grim composure, and substantial, reflective methods of her New England life, the *abandon* and unthinkingness of these French-Canadians were bewildering and delightful to her.

"The whole town is every night like a Sunday-school picnic in our country," she said once to Father Antoine. "What children all these people are!"

"Yes, daughter, it is so," replied the priest; "and it is well. Does not our good Lord say that we cannot enter into His kingdom except we become as little children?"

"Yes, I know," replied Hetty; "but I don't believe this is exactly what he meant, do you?"

"A part of what he meant," answered the priest; "not all. First, docility; and, second, joy: that is what the Church teaches."

"Your Church is better than ours in that respect," said Hetty candidly: "ours doesn't teach joy; it is pretty much all terror."

"Should a child know terror of its mother?" asked Father Antoine. "The Church is mother, and the Holy Virgin is mother. Ah, daughter! it will be a glad day when I see you in the beautiful sheltering arms."

Tears sometimes came to Hetty's eyes at such words as these; and good Father Antoine went with renewed fervor to his prayers for her conversion.

In the centre of the village was a square laid out in winding paths, and surrounded by fir trees. In the middle of this square was a great stone basin, in which a spring perpetually bubbled up; the basin had a broad brim, on which the villagers sat when they came of an evening to fill jugs and bottles with the water. On a bright summer night, the circle would often widen and widen, by men throwing themselves on the ground; children toddling from knee to knee; groups standing in eager talk here and there, until it seemed as if the whole village were gathered around the spring. These were the times when all the village affairs were discussed, and all the village gossip retailed from neighbor to neighbor. The scene was as gay and picturesque as you might see in a little town of Brittany; and the jargon of the Canadian *patois* much more confusing than any dialect one would hear on French soil. Hetty's New England tongue utterly refused to learn this new mode of speech; but her quick and retentive ear soon learned its meanings sufficiently to follow the people in their talk. She often made one of this evening circle at the spring, and it was a pleasant sight to see the quick stir of welcome with which her approach was observed.

" Here comes the good Aunt Hibba from the

Doctor's House," and mothers would push children away, and gossips would crowd, and men would stand up, all to make room for Hetty: then they would gather about her, and those who could speak English would translate for those who could not; and everybody would have something to tell her. It was an odd thing that lovers sought her more than any one else. Many a quarrel Aunt Hibba's good sense healed over; and many a worthless fellow was sent about his business, as he deserved to be, because Aunt Hibba took his sweetheart in hand, and made her see the rights of things. If a traveller, strolling about St. Mary's of a June night, had come upon these chattering groups, and seen how they centred around the sturdy, genial-faced woman, in a straight gray gown and a close white cap, he would have been arrested by the picture at once; and have wondered much who and what Hetty could be: but if you had told him that she was a farmer's daughter from Northern New England, he would have laughed in your face, and said, "Nonsense! she belongs to some of the Orders." Very emphatically would he have said this, if it had chanced to be on one of the evenings when Father Antoine was walking by Hetty's side. Father Antoine knew her custom of lingering at the great spring, and sometimes walked down there at sunset to meet her, to observe her talk with the villagers, and to walk home with her later. Nothing could be stronger proof of the reverence in which the whole village held Hetty, than the fact that it seemed to them all the most fitting and natural thing that she and Father Antoine should stand side by side speaking to the people, should walk away side by side in earnest conversation with each other. If any man had ventured upon a jest or a ribald word concerning them, a dozen quick hands would have given him a plunge headforemost into the great stone basin, which was the commonest expression of popular indignation in St. Mary's; a practice which, strangely enough, did not appear to interfere with anybody's relish of the waters.

Father Antoine had an old servant woman, Marie, who had lived in the Ladeau family since before he was born. She had been by the deathbed of his mother, his father, his grandmother, and of an uncle who had died at some German watering-place: wherever a Ladeau was in any need of service, thither hasted Marie; and if the need were from illness, Marie was all the happier; to lie like a hound on the floor all night, and watch by a sick and suffering Ladeau, was to Marie joy. When the young Antoine had set out for the wildernesses of North America, Marie had prayed to be allowed to come with him; and when he refused she had wept till she fell ill. At the last moment he relented, and bore the poor creature on board ship, wondering within himself if he would be able to keep her alive in the forests. But as soon as there was work to do for him she revived; and all these years she had kept his house, and cared for him as if he were her son. From the day of Hetty's first arrival, old Marie had adopted her into her affections: no one, not born a Ladeau, ever had won such liking from Marie. Much to Hetty's embarrassment, whenever she met her, she insisted on kissing her hand, after the fashion of the humble servitors of great houses in France. Probably, in all these long years of solitary service with Father Antoine, Marie had pined for the sight of some one of her own sex, to whom she could give allegiance, for she was fond of telling long stories about the beautiful ladies of the house of Ladeau; and how she had attired them for balls, and had seen them ride away with cavaliers. There was neither splendor nor beauty in Hetty to attract Marie's fancy;

but Marie had a religious side to her nature, almost as strong as the worldly and passionate one. She saw in Hetty's labors an exaltation of devotion which reminded her of noble ladies who had done penances and taken pilgrimages in her own country. Father Antoine's friendship for Hetty, so unlike any thing Marie had seen him feel towards any woman he had met in these wilds, also stimulated her fancy.

"Ah! but it is good that he has at last a friend to whom he may speak as a Ladeau should speak. May the saints keep her! she has the good heart of one the Virgin loves," said Marie, and many a candle did she buy and keep burning on the convent's shrines for Hetty's protection and conversion.

One night Marie overheard Father Antoine say to Hetty, as he bade her good-night at the garden gate:

"My daughter, you look better and younger every day."

"Do I?" replied Hetty, cheerfully: "that's an odd thing for a woman so old as I am. My birthday is next month. I shall be forty-six."

"Youth is not a matter of years," replied Father Antoine. "I have known very young women much older than you."

Hetty smiled sadly, and walked on. Father Antoine's words had given her a pang. They were almost the same words which Dr. Eben had said to her again and again, when she had reasoned with him against his love for her, a woman so much older than himself. "That is all very well to say," thought Hetty in her matter-of-fact way, "and no doubt there are great differences in people: but old age is old age, soften it how you will; and youth is youth; and youth is beautiful, and old age is ugly. Father Antoine knows it just as well as any man. Don't I see, good as he is, every day of my life, with what a different look he blesses the fair young maidens from that with which he blesses the wrinkled old women. There is no use minding it. It can't be helped. But things might as well be called by their right names."

Marie sat down on a garden bench, and reflected. So the good Aunt Hibba's birthday was next month, and there would be nobody to keep it for her in this strange country. "How can we find out?" thought Marie, "and give her a pleasure."

In summer weather, Father Antoine took his simple dinners on the porch. It was cool there, and the vines and flowers gave to the little nook a certain air of elegance which Father Antoine enjoyed without recognizing why. On this evening Marie lingered after she had removed the table. She fidgeted about, picking up a leaf here and there, and looking at her master, till he perceived that she had something on her mind.

"What is it, Marie?" he asked.

"Oh, M'sieur Antoine!" she replied, "it is about the good Aunt Hibba's birthday. Could you not ask her when is the day? and it should be a *fête* day, if we only knew it; there is not one that would not be glad to help make it beautiful."

"Eh, my Marie, what is it then that you plan? The people in the country from which she comes have no *fêtes*. It might be that she would think it a folly," answered Father Antoine, by no means sure that Hetty would like such a testimonial.

"All the more, then, she would like it," said Marie. "I have watched her. It is delight to her when they dance about the spring, and she has the great love for flowers."

So Father Antoine, by a little circumlocution, discovered when the birthday would come, and told Marie; and Marie began straightway to go back and forth in the village, with a pleased air of mystery.

XIV.

THE birthday fell on a day in June. It so happened that Hetty was later than usual in leaving her patients that night; and her purpose had been to go home by the nearest way, and not pass through the Square. The villagers had feared this, and had forestalled her; at the turning where she would have left the main road, she found waiting for her the swiftest-footed urchin in all St. Mary's, little Pierre Michaud. The readiest witted, too, and of the freest tongue, and he was charged to bring Aunt Hibba by the way of the Square, but by no means to tell her the reason.

"And if she say me nay, what is it that I am to tell her, then?" urged Pierrre.

"Art thou a fool, Pierre?" said his mother, sharply. "Thou 'rt ready enough with excuses, I 'll warrant, for thy own purposes: invent one now. It matters not, so that thou bring her here." And Pierre, reassured by this maternal *carte blanche* for the best lie he could think of, raced away, first tucking securely into a niche of the stone basin the little pot with a red carnation in it which he had brought for his contribution to the birthday *fête*.

When Hetty saw Pierre waiting at the corner, she exclaimed:

"What, Pierre, loitering here! The sunset is no time to idle. Where are your goats?"

"Milked an hour ago, Tantibba,* and in the shed," replied Pierre, with a saucy air of having the best of the argument, "and my mother waits in the Square to speak to thee as thou passest."

"I was not going that way, to-night," replied Hetty. "I am in haste. What does she wish? Will it not do as well in the morning?"

Alarmed at this suggestion, young Pierre made a master-stroke of invention, and replied on the instant:

"Nay, Bo Tantibba,† that it will not; for it is the little sister of Jean Cochot which has been badly bitten by a fierce dog, and the mother has her there in her arms waiting for thee to dress

---

* "Tante Hibba."

† The French Canadians often contract "bonne" and "bon" in this way. "Bo Tantibba" is contraction for "Bonne Tante Hibba."

her wounds. Oh, but the blood doth run! and the little one's cries would pierce thy heart!" And the rascally Pierre pretended to sob.

"Eh, eh, how happened that?" said Hetty, hurrying on so swiftly towards the Square that even Pierre's brisk little legs could hardly keep up with her. Pierre's inventive faculty came to a halt.

"Nay, that I do not know," he replied; "but the people are all gathered around her, and they all cry out for thee by thy name. There is none like thee, Tantibba, they say, if one has a wound."

Hetty quickened her pace to a run. As she entered the Square, she saw such crowds around the basin that Pierre's tale seemed amply corroborated. Pressing in at the outer edge of the circle, she exclaimed, looking to right and left, "Where is the child? Where is Mère Michaud?" Every one looked bewildered; no one answered. Pierre, with an upward fling of his agile legs, disappeared to seek his carnation; and Hetty found herself, in an instant more, surrounded by a crowd of children, each in its finest clothes, and each bearing a small pot with a flowering-plant in it.

"For thee! For thee! The good saints bless the day thou wert born!" they all cried, pressing nearer, and lifting high their little pots.

"See my carnation!" shouted Pierre, struggling nearer to Hetty. "And my jonquil!" "And my pansies!" "And this forget-me-not!" cried the children, growing more and more excited each moment; while the chorus, "For thee! For thee! The good saints bless the day thou wert born!" rose on all sides.

Hetty was bewildered.

"What does all this mean?" she said helplessly.

Then, catching Pierre by the shoulder so suddenly that his red carnation tottered and nearly fell, she exclaimed:

"You mischievous boy! Where is the child that was bitten? Have you told me a lie?"

At this moment, Pierre's mother, pushing through the crowd, exclaimed:

"Ah! but thou must forgive him. It was I that sent him to lie to thee, that thou shouldst not go home. We go with thee, to do our honor to the day on which thou wert born!"

And so saying, Mère Michaud turned, and swinging high up in the air one end of a long wreath of feathery ground-pine, led off the procession. The rest followed in preconcerted order, till some forty men and women, all linked together by the swinging loops of the pine wreath, were in line. Then they suddenly wheeled and surrounded the bewildered Hetty, and bore her with them. The children, carrying their little pots of flowers, ran along shouting and screaming with laughter to see the good "Tantibba" so amazed. Louder and louder rose the chorus:

"For thee! For thee! May the good saints bless the day thou wert born!"

Hetty was speechless: her cheeks flushed. She looked from one to the other, and all she could do was to clasp her hands and smile. If she had spoken, she would have cried. When they came to Father Antoine's cottage, there he stood waiting at the gate, wearing his Sunday robes, and behind him stood Marie, also in her best, and with her broad silver necklace on, which the villagers had only two or three times seen her wear. Marie had her hands behind her, and was trying to hold out her narrow black petticoat on each side to hide something. Mysterious and plaintive noises struggled through the woollen folds, and, at each sound, Marie stamped her foot and exclaimed angrily:

"Bah! thou silly beast, be quiet! Wilt thou spoil all our sport?"

The procession halted before the house, and Father Antoine advanced, bearing in his hands a gay wreath of flowers. The people had wished that this should be placed on Hetty's head, but Father Antoine had persuaded them to waive this part of the ceremony. He knew well that this would be more than Hetty could bear. Holding the wreath in his hands, therefore, he addressed a few words to Hetty, and then took his place by her side. Now was Marie's moment of joy. Springing to one side as quickly as her rheumatic old joints would permit, she revealed what she had been trying to hide behind her scant petticoat. It was a white lamb, decorated from ears to tail with knots of ribbon and with flowers. The poor little thing tugged hard at the string by which it was held, and shook its pretty head in restless impatience under its load of finery, and bleated piteously: but for all that it was a very pretty sight; and the broken English with which Marie, on behalf of the villagers, presented the little creature to Hetty, was prettier still. When they reached Hetty's gate, all the women who had hold of the long pine wreath gave their places to men; and, in the twinkling of an eye, the lithe vigorous fellows were on the fences, on the posts of the porch, nailing the wreath in festoons everywhere; from the gateway to the door in long swinging loops, above the porch, in festoons over the windows, under the eaves, and hanging in long waving ends on the walls. Then they hung upon the door the crown which Hetty had not worn, and the little children set their gay pots of flowers on the window-sills and around the porch ; and all was a merry hubbub of voices and laughter. Hetty grasped Father Antoine by the arm.

"Oh, do you speak to them, and thank them for me! I can't!" she said ; and Father Antoine saw tears in her eyes.

"But you must speak to them, my daughter," he replied, "else they will be grieved. They cannot understand that you are pleased if you say no word. I will speak first till you are more calm."

When Father Antoine had finished his speech, Hetty stepped forward, and looking round on all their faces, said :

"I do not know how to thank you, friends. I never saw any thing like this before, and it makes me dumb. All I can say is that you have filled my heart with joy, and I feel no more a stranger : your village is my home."

"Thanks to thee, then, for that! Thanks to thee! And the good saints bless the day thou wert born," shouted the people, and the little children catching the enthusiasm, and wanting to shout something, shouted: "Bo Tantibba! Bo Tantibba!" till the place rang. Then they placed the pet lamb in a little enclosed paddock which had been built for him during the day, and the children fed him with red clover blossoms through the paling; and presently, Father Antoine considerately led his flock away, saying,— "The good Aunt is weary. See you not that her eyes droop, and she has no words? It is now kind that we go away, and leave her to rest."

As the gay procession moved away crying, "Good-night, good-night!" Hetty stood on the porch and watched them. She was on the point of calling them back. A strange dread of being left alone seized upon her. Never since she had forsaken her home had she felt such a sense of loneliness, except when she was crouched under the hemlock-trees by the lake. She watched till she could no longer see even a fluttering motion in the distance. Then she went into the house. The silence smote her. She turned and went out again, and went to the paddock, where the little lamb was bleating.

"Poor little creature!" she said, "wert thou torn from thy mother? Dost thou pine for one thou see'st not?" She untied it, led it into the house, and spread down hay and blankets for it, in one corner of her kitchen. The little creature seemed cheered by the light and warmth; cuddled down and went to sleep.

Hetty's heart was full of thoughts. "Oh! what would Eben have said if he could have seen me to-night?" "How Raby would have delighted in it all!" "How long am I to live this strange life?" "Can this be really I?" "What has become of my old life, of my old self?" Like restless waves driven by a wind too powerful to be resisted, thoughts and emotions surged through Hetty's breast. She buried her face in her hands and wept; wept the first unrestrained tears she had wept. Only for a few moments, however. Like the old Hetty Gunn of the old life, she presently sprang to her feet, and said to herself, "Oh, what a selfish soul I am to be spending all my strength this way! I shan't be fit for any thing to-morrow if I go on so." Then she patted the lamb on its head, and said with a comforting sense of comradeship in the little creature's presence, "Good-night, little motherless one! Sleep warm," and then she went to bed and slept till morning.

I have dwelt on the surface details of Hetty's

life at St. Mary's, and have said little about her mental condition and experiences: this is because I have endeavored to present this part of her life, exactly as she lived it, and as she would tell it herself. That there were many hours of acute suffering; many moments when her courage wellnigh failed; when she was almost ready to go back to her home, fling herself at her husband's feet, and cry, "Let me be but as a servant in thy house,"—it is not needful to say.

Hearts answer to hearts, and no heart could fail to know that a woman in Hetty's position must suffer keenly and constantly. But this story would do great injustice to her, and would be essentially false, if it spoke often of, or dwelt at any length upon the sufferings which Hetty herself never mentioned, and put always away from her with an unflinching resolution. Year after year, the routine of her days went on as we have described; unchanged except that she grew more and more into the affections of the villagers among whom she came and went, and of the hundreds of ill and suffering men and women whom she nursed. She was no nearer becoming a Roman Catholic than she had been when she sat in the Welbury meeting-house: even Father Antoine had given over hoping for her conversion; but her position in St. Mary's was like the position of a Lady Abbess in a religious community; her authority, which rarely took on an authoritative shape, was great; and her influence was greater than her authority. In Dr. Macgowan's House of Cure, she was second only to the doctor himself; and, if the truth were told, it might have been said she was second to none.

Patients went away from St. Mary's every year who stoutly ascribed their cure to her, and not to the waters nor to the physicians. Her straightforward, kindly, common sense was a powerful tonic, morally and physically, to all invalids whom she nursed. She had no tolerance for any weakness which could be conquered. She had infinite tenderness for all weakness which was inevitable; and her discriminations between the two were always just. "I'd trust more to Mrs. Smailli's diagnosis of any case than I would to my own," said Dr. Macgowan to his fellow-physicians more than once. And, when they scoffed at the idea, he replied: "I do not mean in the technicalities of specific disease, of course. The recognition of those is a matter of specific training; but, in all those respects, a physician's diagnosis may be faultless; and yet he be much mistaken in regard to the true condition of the patient. In this finer, subtler diagnosis of general conditions, especially of moral conditions, Mrs. Smailli is worth more than all the doctors in Canada put together. If she says a patient will get well, he always does, and *vice versa*. She knows where the real possibility of recuperation lies, and detects it often in patients I despair of."

XV.

AND now this story must again pass over a period of ten years in the history of Eben and Hetty Williams. During all these years, Hetty had been working faithfully in St. Mary's; and Dr. Eben had been working faithfully in Welbury. Hetty was now fifty-six years old. Her hair was white, and clustered round her temples in a rim of snowy curls, peeping out from under the close lace cap she always wore. But the snowy curls were hardly less becoming than the golden brown ones had been. Her cheeks were still pink, and her lips red. She looked far less old for her age at fifty-six than she had looked ten years before.

Dr. Eben, on the other hand, had grown old fast. His work had not been to him as complete and healthful occupation as Hetty's had been to her. He had lived more within himself; and he had never ceased to sorrow. His sorrow, being for one dead, was without hope;

save that intangible hope to which our faith so pathetically clings, of the remote and undefined possibilities of eternity. Hetty's sorrow was full of hope, being persuaded that all was well with those whom she did not see.

Dr. Eben loved no one warmly or with absorption. Hetty loved every suffering one to whom she ministered. Dr. Eben had never ceased living too much in the past. Hetty had learned to live almost wholly in the present. Hetty had suffered, had suffered intensely; but all that she had suffered was as nothing in comparison with the sufferings of her husband. Moreover, Hetty had kept through all these years her superb health. Dr. Eben had had severe illnesses, which had told heavily upon his strength. From all these things it had come to pass, that now he looked older and more worn than Hetty. She looked vigorous; he looked feeble; she was still comely, he had lost all the fineness of color and outline, which had made him at forty so handsome a man. He had been growing restless, too, and discontented.

Raby was away at college; old Cæsar and Nan had both died, and their places were filled by new white servants, who, though they served

Dr. Eben well, did not love him. Deacon Little had died also, and Jim and Sally had been obliged to go back to the old homestead to live, to take care of Mrs. Little, who was now a helpless paralytic.

"Gunn's," as it was still called, and always would be, was no longer the brisk and cheerful place which it had once been. The farm was slowly falling off, from its master's lack of interest in details; and the old stone house had come to wear a certain look of desolation. The pines met and interlaced their boughs over the whole length of the road from the gate to the front-door; and, in a dark day, it was like an underground passage-way, cold and damp. If Hetty could have been transported to the spot, how would her heart have ached! How would she have seen, in terrible handwriting, the record of her mistaken act; the blight which her one wrong step had cast, not only upon hearts and lives, but even upon the visible face of nature. But Hetty did not dream of this. Whenever she permitted her fancy to dwell upon imaginings of her old home, she saw it bright with sunshine, merry with the voices of little children: and her husband handsome still, and young, walking by the side of a beautiful woman, mother of his children.

At last Dr. Eben took a sudden resolution; the result, partly, of his restless discontent; partly of his consciousness that he was in danger of breaking down and becoming a chronic invalid. He offered "Gunn's" for sale, and announced that he was going abroad for some years. Spite of the dismay with which this news was received throughout the whole county, everybody's second thought was: "Poor fellow! I'm glad of it. It's the best thing he can do."

Hetty's cousin, Josiah Gunn, the man that she had so many years ago predicted would ultimately have the estate, bought it in, outbidding the most determined bidders (for " Gunn's " was much coveted); and paying finally a sum even larger than the farm was really worth. Dr. Eben was now a rich man, and free. The world lay before him. When all was done, he felt a strange unwillingness to leave Welbury. The travel, the change, which had looked so desirable and attractive, now looked formidable; and he lingered week after week, unable to tear himself away from home. One day he rode over to Springton, to bid Rachel Barlow good-by. Rachel was now twenty-eight years old, and a very beautiful woman. Many men had sought to marry her, but Dr. Eben's prediction had been realized. Rachel would not marry. Her health was perfectly established, and she had been for years at the head of the Springton Academy. Doctor Eben rarely saw her; but when he did her manner had the same child-like docility and affectionate gratitude that had characterized it when she was seventeen. She had never ceased to feel that she owed her life, and more than her life, to him: how much more she felt, Dr. Eben had never dreamed until this day. When he told her that he was going to Europe, she turned pale, but said earnestly:

"Oh, I am very glad! you have needed the change so much. How long will you stay?"

"I don't know, Rachel," he replied sadly. "Perhaps all the rest of my life. I have done my best to live here; but I can't. It's no use: I can't bear it. I have sold the place."

Rachel's lips parted, but she did not speak; her face flushed scarlet, then turned white; and, without a moment's warning or possibility of staying the tears, she buried her face in her hands, and wept convulsively. In the same instant, a magnetic sense of all that this grief meant thrilled through Doctor Eben's every nerve. No such thought had ever crossed his mind before. Rachel had never been to him any thing but the "child" he had first called her. Very reverently seeking now to shield her womanhood from any after pain of fear, lest she might have betrayed her secret, he said:

"Why, my child! you must not feel so badly about it. I ought not to have spoken so. Of course, you must know that my life has been a very lonely one, and always must be. But I should not give up and go away, simply for that. I am not well, and I am quite sure that I need several years of a milder climate. I dare say I shall be home-sick, and come back after all."

Rachel lifted her eyes and looked steadily in his. Her tears stopped. The old clairvoyant gaze, which he had not seen on her face for many years, returned.

"No. You will never come back," she said slowly. Then, as one speaking in a dream, she said still more slowly, and uttering each word with difficulty and emphasis:

"I — do — not — believe — your — wife — is — dead." Much shocked, and thinking that these words were merely the utterance of an hysterical excitement, Dr. Eben replied:

"Not to me, dear child; she never will be: but

you must not let yourself be excited in this way. You will be ill. I must be your doctor again and prescribe for you."

Rachel continued to watch him, with the same bright and unflinching gaze. He turned from her, and, bringing her a glass of water in which he had put a few drops from a vial, said in his old tone:

"Drink this, Rachel."

She obeyed in silence; her eyes drooped; the tension of her whole figure relaxed; and, with a long sigh, she exclaimed:

"Oh, forgive me!"

"There is nothing to forgive, my child," said the doctor, much moved, and, longing to throw his arms around her as she sat there, so gentle, appealing, beautiful, loving. "Why can I not love her?" "What else is there better in life for me to do?" he thought, but his heart refused. Hetty, the lost dead Hetty, stood as much between him and all other women to-day, as she had stood ten years before.

"I must go now, Rachel," he said. "Good-by."

She put her cold hand in his. As he took it, by a curious freak of his brain, there flashed into his mind the memory of the day when, by the side of this fragile white little hand lying in his, Hetty, laughingly, had placed her own, broad and firm and brown. The thought of that hand of Hetty's, and her laugh at that moment, were too much for him, and he dropped Rachel's hand abruptly, and moved toward the door. She gave a low cry: he turned back; she took a step towards him.

"I shall never see you again," she said, taking his hand in hers. "I owe my life to you," and she carried his hand to her lips, and kissed it again and again. "God bless you, child! Good-by! good-by!" he said. Rachel did not speak, and he left her standing there, gazing after him with a look on her face which haunted him as long as he lived.

Why Doctor Eben should have resolved to sail for England in a Canadian steamer, and why, having reached Canada, he should have resolved to postpone his voyage, and make a trial of the famous springs of St. Mary's, are mysteries hid in that book of Fate whose leaves no mortal may turn. We prate in our shallow wisdom about causes, but the most that we can trace is a short line of incidental occasions. A pamphlet which Doctor Eben found in the office of a hotel was apparently the reason of his going to St. Mary's; all the reason so far as he knew, or as any man might know. But that man is to be pitied who lives his life out under the impression that it is within his own guidance. Only one remove from the life of the leaf which the winds toss where they list would be such a life as that.

It was with no very keen interest that Doctor Eben arrived in St. Mary's. He had some faint hope that the waters might do him good: but he found the sandy stretches and long lines of straight firs in Canada very monotonous; and he was already beginning to be oppressed by the sense of homelessness. His quiet and domestic life had unfitted him for being a wanderer, and he was already looking forward to the greater excitements of European travel; hoping that they would prove more diverting and entertaining than he had thus far found travel in America.

He entered St. Mary's as Hetty had done, just at sunset. It was a warm night in June; and, after his tea at the little inn, Dr. Eben sauntered out listlessly. The sound of merry voices in the Square repelled him; unlike Hetty, he shrank from strange faces: turning in the direction where it seemed stillest, he walked slowly towards the woods. He looked curiously at the little red chapel, and at Father Antoine's cottage, now literally imbedded in flowers. Then he paused before Hetty's tiny house. A familiar fragrance arrested him; leaning on the paling he looked over into the garden, started, and said, under his breath: "How strange! How strange!" There were long straight beds of lavender and balm, growing together, as they used to grow in the old garden at "Gunn's." Both the balm and the lavender were in full blossom; and the two scents mingled and separated and mingled in the warm air, like the notes of two instruments unlike, yet in harmony. The strong lemon odor of the balm, was persistently present like the mastering chords of the violoncello, and the fine and subtle fragrances from the myriad cells of the pale lavender floated above and below, now distant, now melting and disappearing, like a delicate melody. Dr. Eben was borne away from the present, out of himself. He thrust his hand through the palings, and gathered a crushed handful of the lavender blossoms: eagerly he inhaled their perfume. Drawers and chests at "Gunn's" had been thick strewn with lavender for half a century. All Hetty's clothes — Hetty herself — had been full of the exquisite fragrance. The sound of quick pattering steps roused him from his reverie. A bare-footed boy was driving a flock of goats past. The child stopped and gazed intently at the stranger.

"Child, who lives in this little house?" said Dr. Eben, cautiously hiding his stolen handful of lavender.

"Tantibba," replied the boy.

"What!" exclaimed the doctor. "I don't understand you. What is the name?"

"Tantibba! Tantibba!" the child shouted, looking back over his shoulder, as he raced on to overtake his goats. "Bo Tantibba." "Some old French name I suppose," thought Dr. Eben: "but, it is very odd about the herbs; the two growing together, so exactly as Hetty used to have them;" and he walked reluctantly away, carrying the bruised lavender blossoms in his hand, and breathing in their delicious fragrance. As he drew near the inn, he observed on the other side of the way a woman hurrying in the opposite direction. She had a sturdy thick-set figure, and her step, although rapid, was not the step of a young person. She wore on her head only a close white cap; and her gray gown was straight and scant: on her arm she carried a basket of scarlet plaited straw, which made a fine bit of color against the gray and white of her costume. It was just growing dusk, and the doctor could not distinguish her features. At that moment, a lad came running from the inn, and darted across the road, calling aloud, "Tantibba! Tantibba!" The woman turned her head, at the name, and waited till the lad came to her. Dr. Eben stood still, watching them. "So that is Tantibba?" he thought, "what can the name be?" Presently the lad came back with a bunch of long drooping balm-stalks in his hand.

"Who was that you spoke to then?" asked the doctor.

"Tantibba!" replied the lad, hurrying on. Dr. Eben caught him by the shoulder. "Look here!" he exclaimed, "just tell me that name again. This is the fourth time I've heard it to-night. Is it the woman's first name or what?" The lad was a stupid English lad, who had but recently come to service in St. Mary's, and had never even thought to wonder what the name "Tantibba," meant. He stared vacantly for a moment, and then said:

"Indeed, sir, and I don't know. She's never called any thing else that I've heard."

"Who is she? what does she do?" asked the doctor.

"Oh, sir! she's a great nurse, from foreign parts: she has a power of healing-herbs in her garden, and she goes each day to the English House to heal the sick. There's nobody like her. If she do but lay her hand on one, they do say it is a cure."

"She is French, I suppose," said the doctor; thinking to himself, "Some adventuress, doubtless."

"Ay, sir, I think so," answered the lad; "but I must not stay to speak any more, for the mistress waits for this balm to make tea for the cook Jean, who is like to have a fever;" and the lad disappeared under the low archway of the basement.

Dr. Eben walked back and forth in front of the inn, still crushing in his fingers the lavender flowers and inhaling their fragrance. Idly he watched "Tantibba's" figure till it disappeared in the distance.

"This is just the sort of place for a tricky old French woman to make a fortune in," he said to himself: "these people are simple enough to believe any thing;" and Dr. Eben went to his room, and tossed the lavender blossoms down on his pillow.

When he waked in the morning, his first thoughts were bewildered: nothing in nature is so powerful in association as a perfume. A sound, a sight, is feeble in comparison; the senses are ever alert, and the mind is accustomed always to act promptly on their evidence. But a subtle perfume, which has been associated with a person, a place, a scene, can ever afterward arrest us; can take us unawares, and hold us spell-bound, while both memory and knowledge are drugged by its charm.

Dr. Eben did not open his eyes. In an ecstasy of half consciousness he murmured, "Hetty." As he stirred, his hand came in contact with the withered flowers. Touch was more potent than smell. He roused, lifted his head, saw the little blossoms now faded and gray lying near his cheek; and saying, "Oh, I remember," sank back again into a few moments' drowsy reverie.

The morning was clear and cool, one window of the doctor's room looked east; the splendor of the sunrise shone in and illuminated the whole place. While he was dressing, he found himself persistently thinking of the strange name, "Tantibba." "It is odd how that name haunts me," he thought. "I wish I could see it written: I haven't the least idea how it is spelled. I wonder if she is an impostor. Her garden didn't look like it." Presently he sauntered out: the morning stir was just beginning in the village. The child to whom he had spoken at "Tantibba's" gate, the night before, came up, driving the same flock of goats. The little fellow, as he passed, pulled the ragged tassel of his cap in token of recognition of the stranger who had accosted him. Without any definite purpose, Dr. Eben followed slowly on, watching a pair of young kids, who fell behind the flock, frolicking and half-fighting in antics so grotesque that they looked more like gigantic grasshoppers than like goats. Before he knew how far he had walked, he suddenly perceived that he was very near "Tantibba's" house.

"I'll walk on and steal another handful of the lavender," he thought; "and if the old woman's up, perhaps I'll get a sight of her. I'd like to see what sort of a face answers to that outlandish name."

As the doctor leaned over the paling, and looked again at Hetty's garden, he saw something which had escaped his notice before, and at which he started again, and muttered — this time aloud, and with an expression almost of terror, — "Good Heavens, if there isn't a chrysanthemum bed too, exactly like ours! what does this mean?" Hetty had little thought when she was laying out her garden, as nearly as possible like the garden she had left behind her, that she was writing a record which any eye but her own would note.

"I believe I'll go in and see this old French woman," he thought: "it is such a strange thing that she should have just the same flowers Hetty had. I don't believe she's an adventuress, after all."

Dr. Eben had his hand on the latch of the gate. At that instant, the cottage door opened, and "Tantibba," in her white cap and gray gown, and with her scarlet basket on her arm, appeared on the threshold. Dr. Eben lifted his hat courteously, and advanced.

"I was just about to take the liberty of knocking at your door, madame," he said, "to ask if you would give me a few of your lavender blossoms."

As he began to speak, "Tantibba's" basket fell from her hand. As he advanced towards her, her eyes grew large with terror, and all color left her cheeks.

"Why do I terrify her so?" thought Dr. Eben, quickening his steps, and hastening to reassure her, by saying still more gently:

"Pray forgive me for intruding. I" — the

words died on his lips: he stood like one stricken by paralysis; his hands falling helplessly by his side, and his eyes fixed in almost ghastly dread on this gray-haired woman, from whose white lips came, in Hetty's voice, the cry:

"Eben! oh! Eben!"

Hetty was the first to recover herself. Seeing with terror how rigid and pale her husband's face had become; how motionless, like one turned to stone, he stood — she hastened down the steps, and, taking him by the hand, said, in a trembling whisper:

"Oh, come into the house, Eben."

Mechanically he followed her; she still leading him by the hand, like a child. Like a child, or rather like a blind man, he sat down in the chair which she placed for him. His eyes did not move from her face; but they looked almost like sightless eyes. Hetty stood before him, with her hands clasped tight. Neither spoke. At last Dr. Eben said feebly:

"Are you Hetty?"

"Yes, Eben," answered Hetty, with a tearless sob. He did not speak again: still with a strange unseeing look, his eyes roved over her face, her figure. Then he reached out one hand and touched her gown; curiously, he lifted the soft gray serge, and fingered it; then he said again:

"Are you Hetty?"

"Oh, Eben! dear Eben! indeed I am," broke forth Hetty. "Do forgive me. Can't you?"

"Forgive you?" repeated Dr. Eben, helplessly. "What for?"

"Oh, my God! he thinks we are both dead: what shall I do to rouse him?" thought Hetty, all the nurse in her coming to the rescue of the woman and wife.

"For going away and leaving you, Eben," she said in a clear resolute voice. "I wasn't drowned. I came away."

Dr. Eben smiled; a smile which terrified Hetty more than his look or voice or words had done.

"Eben! Eben!" she cried, putting both her hands on his shoulders, and bringing her face close to his. "Don't look like that. I tell you I wasn't drowned. I am alive: feel me! feel me! I am Hetty;" and she knelt before him, and laid her arms across his knees. The touch, the grasp, the warmth of her strong flesh, penetrated his inmost consciousness, and brought back the tottering senses. His eyes lost their terrifying and ghastly expression, and took on one searching and half-stern.

"You were not drowned!" he said. "You have not been dead all these years! You went away! You are not Hetty!" and he pushed her arms rudely from his knees. Then, in the next second, he had clasped her fiercely in his arms, crying aloud :

"You are Hetty! I feel you! I know you! Oh Hetty, Hetty, wife, what does this all mean? Who took you away from me?" And tears, blessed saving tears, filled Dr. Eben's eyes.

Now began the retribution of Hetty's mistake. In this moment, with her husband's arms around her, his eyes fixed on hers, the whole cloud of misapprehension under which she had acted was revealed to her as by a beam of divine light from heaven. Smitten to the heart by a sudden and overwhelming remorse, Hetty was speechless. She could only look pleadingly into his face, and murmur:

"Oh, Eben! Eben!"

He repeated his questions, growing calmer with each word, and with each moment's increasing realization of Hetty's presence.

"Who took you away?"

"Nobody," answered Hetty. "I came alone."

"Did you not love me, Hetty?" said Dr. Eben in sad tones, struck by a new fear.

This question unsealed Hetty's lips.

"Love you!" she exclaimed in a piercing voice. "Love you! oh, Eben!" and then she poured out, without reserves or disguises, the whole story of her convictions, her decision, and her flight. Her husband did not interrupt her by word or gesture. As she proceeded with her narrative, he slowly withdrew his eyes from her face, and fixed them on the floor. It was harder for her to speak when he thus looked away from her. Timidly she said:

"Do not turn your eyes away from me, Eben. It makes me afraid. I cannot tell you the rest, if you look so."

With an evident effort, he raised his eyes again, and again met her earnest gaze. But it was only for a few seconds. Again his eyes drooped, evaded hers, and rested on the floor. Again Hetty paused; and said still more pleadingly:

"Please look at me, Eben. Indeed I can't talk to you if you do not."

Like one stung suddenly by some insupportable pain, he wrenched her hands from his knees, sprang to his feet, and walked swiftly back and forth. She remained kneeling by the chair, looking up at him with a most piteous face.

"Hetty," he exclaimed, "you must be patient with me. Try and imagine what it is to have believed for ten years that you were dead; to have mourned you as dead; to have spent ten whole years of weary, comfortless days; and then to find suddenly that you have been all this time living, — voluntarily hiding yourself from me; needlessly torturing me! Why, Hetty! Hetty! you must have been mad. You must be mad now, I think, to kneel there and tell me all these details so calmly, and in such a matter-of-fact way. Do you realize what a monstrous thing you have been doing?" And Dr. Eben's eyes blazed with a passionate indignation, as he stopped short in his excited walk and looked down upon Hetty. Then, in the next second, touched by the look on her uplifted face, so noble, so pure, so benevolent, he forgot all his resentment, all his perplexity, all his pain; and, stooping over her, he lifted her from her knees, and, folding her close to his bosom, exclaimed:

"Oh, my Hetty, my own; forgive me. I am the one that is mad. How can I think of any thing except the joy of having found you again? No wonder I thought at first we were both dead. Oh, my precious wife, is it really you? Are you sure we are alive?" And he kissed her again and again, — hair, brow, eyes, lips, — with a solemn rapture.

A great silence fell upon them: there seemed no more to say. Suddenly, Dr. Eben exclaimed:

"Rachel said she did not believe you were dead."

At mention of Rachel's name, a spasm crossed Hetty's face. In the excitement of her mingled terror and joy, she had not yet thought of Rachel.

"Where is Rachel?" she gasped, her very heart standing still as she asked the question.

"At home," answered the doctor; and his countenance clouded at the memory of his last interview with her. Hetty's fears misinterpreted the reply and the sudden cloud on his face.

"Is she — did you — where is her home?" she stammered.

A great light broke in on Dr. Eben's mind.

"Good God!" he cried. "Hetty, it is not possible that you thought I loved Rachel?"

"No," said Hetty. "I only thought you could love her, if it were right; and if I were dead it would be."

A look of horror deepened on the doctor's

face. The idea thus suggested to his mind was terrible.

"And supposing I had loved her, thinking you were dead, what then? Do you know what you would have done?" he said sternly.

"I think you would have been very happy," replied Hetty, simply. "I have always thought of you as being probably very happy."

Dr. Eben groaned aloud.

"Oh, Hetty! Hetty! How could God have let you think such thoughts? Hetty!" he exclaimed suddenly, with the manner of one who has taken a new resolve: "Hetty, listen. We must not talk about this terrible past. It is impossible for me to be just to you. If any other woman had done what you have done, I should say she must be mad, or else wicked."

"I think I was mad," interrupted Hetty. "It seems so to me now. But, indeed, Eben, oh, indeed, I thought at the time it was right."

"I know you did, my darling," replied the doctor. "I believe it fully; but for all that I cannot be just to you, when I think of it. We must put it away from us for ever. We are old now, and have perhaps only a few years to live together."

Here Hetty interrupted him with a sudden cry of dismay:

"Oh! oh! I forgot every thing but you. I ought to have been at Dr. Macgowan's an hour ago. Indeed, Eben, I must go this minute. Do not try to hinder me. There is a patient there who is so ill. I fear he will not live through the day. Oh, how selfish of me to have forgotten him for a single moment! But how can I leave you! How can I leave you!"

As she spoke, she moved hastily about the room, making her preparations to go. Her husband did not attempt to delay her. A strange feeling was creeping over him, that, by Hetty's removal of herself from him, by her new life, her new name, new duties, she had really ceased to be his. He felt weak and helpless: the shock had been too great, and he was not strong. When Hetty was ready, he said:

"Shall I walk with you, Hetty?"

She hesitated. She feared to be seen talking in an excited way with this stranger: she dreaded to lose her husband out of her sight.

"Oh, Eben!" she exclaimed, "I do not know what to do. I cannot bear to let you go from me for a moment. How shall I get through this day! I will not go to Dr. Macgowan's any more. I will get Sister Catharine from the convent to come and take my place at once. Yes, come with me. We will walk together, but we must not talk, Eben."

"No," said her husband.

He understood and shared her feeling. In silence they took their way through the outskirts of the town. Constantly they stole furtive looks at each other; Hetty noting with sorrow the lines which grief and ill-health had made in the doctor's face; he thinking to himself:

"Surely it is a miracle that age and white hair should make a woman more beautiful."

But it was not the age, the white hair: it was the transfiguration of years of self-sacrifice and ministering to others.

"Hetty," said Dr. Eben, as they drew near Dr. Macgowan's gate, "what is this name by which the village people call you? I heard it on everybody's lips, but I could not make it out."

Hetty colored. "It is French for Aunt Hibba," she replied. "They speak it as if it were one word, 'Tantibba.'"

"But there was more to it," said her husband. "'Bo Tantibba,' they called you."

"Oh, that means merely 'Good Aunt Hibba,'" she said confusedly. "You see some of them think I have been good to them; that's all: but usually they call me only 'Tantibba.'"

"Why did you call yourself 'Hibba'?" he said.

"I don't know," replied Hetty. "It came into my head."

"Don't they know your last name?" asked her husband, earnestly.

"Oh!" said Hetty, "I changed that too."

Dr. Eben stopped short: his face grew stern.

"Hetty," he said, "do you mean to tell me that you have put my very name away from you all these years?"

Tears came to Hetty's eyes.

"Why, Eben," she replied, "what else could I do? It would have been absurd to keep my name. Any day it might have been recognized. Don't you see?"

"Yes, I see," answered Dr. Eben, bitterly. "You are no longer mine, even by name."

Hetty's tears fell. She was dumb before all resentful words, all passionate outbreaks, from her husband now. All she could say was:

"Oh, Eben! Eben!" Sometimes she added piteously: "I never meant to do wrong; at least, no wrong to you. I thought if there were wrong, it would be only to myself, and on my own head."

When they parted, Dr. Eben said:

"At what hour are you free, Hetty?"

"At six," she replied. "Will you wait for me at the house? Do not come here."

"Very well," he answered; and, making a formal salutation as to a stranger, he turned away.

XVI.

WITH a heavy heart, in midst of all her joy, Hetty went about her duties: vague fears oppressed her. What would Eben do now? What had he meant when he said: "You are no longer mine, even in name"?

Now that Hetty perceived that she had been wrong in leaving him; that, instead of providing, as she had hoped she should, for his greater happiness, she had only plunged him into inconsolable grief, — her one desire was to atone for it; to return to him; to be to him, if possible, more than she had ever been. But great timidity and apprehension filled her breast. He seemed to be angry with her. Would he forgive her? Would he take her home? Had she forfeited her right to go home? Hour after hour, as the weary day went on, she tortured herself with these thoughts. Wistfully her patients watched her face. It was impossible for her to conceal her preoccupation and anxiety. At last the slow sun sank behind the fir-trees, and brought her hour of release. Seeking Dr. Macgowan, she told him that she would send Sister Catharine on the next day " to take my place for the present, perhaps altogether," said Hetty.

"Good heavens! Mrs. Smailli!" exclaimed the doctor. "What is the matter? Are you ill? You shall have a rest; but we can't give you up."

"No, I am not ill," replied Hetty, "but circumstances have occurred which make it impossible for me to say what my plans will be now."

"What is it? Bless my soul, what shall we do?" said Dr. Macgowan, looking very much vexed. "Really, Mrs. Smailli, you can't give up your post in this way."

The doctor forgot himself in his dismay.

"I would not leave it, if there were no one to fill it," replied Hetty, gently; "but Sister Catharine is a better nurse than I am. She will more than fill my place."

"Pshaw! Mrs. Smailli," ejaculated the doctor. "She can't hold a candle to you. Is it any thing about the salary which is taking you away? I will raise it: you shall fix your own price."

Flushing red with shame, Hetty said hotly:

"I have never worked for the money, Dr. Macgowan; only for enough for my living. Money has nothing to do with it. Good-morning."

"That's just what comes of depending on women," growled Dr. Macgowan. "They're all alike; no stability to 'em! What under heaven can it be? She's surely too old to have got any idea of marrying into her head. I'll go and see Father Antoine, and see if he can't influence her."

But when Dr. Macgowan, a few days later, reached Father Antoine's cottage, he was met by news which slew on the instant all his hopes of ever seeing Mrs. Hibba Smailli in his House again as a nurse. Hetty and her husband had spent the previous evening with Father Antoine, and had laid their case fully before him. Hetty had given him permission to tell all the facts to Dr. Macgowan, under the strictest pledges of secrecy.

"'Pon my word! 'pon my word!" said the doctor, "the most extraordinary thing I ever heard of! Who'd have thought that calm, clear-headed woman would ever have committed such a folly? It's a case of monomania; a real monomania, Father Antoine; never can be sure of such a brain's that; may take another, any day; clear case of monomania; most uncomfortable! uncomfortable! so embarrassing! don't you know? eh? What's going to be done now? How does the man take it? Is he a gentleman? Hang me, if I wouldn't let a woman stay where she was, that had served me such a trick!"

Father Antoine laughed a low pleasant laugh.

"And that would be by how much you had loved her, is it not?" he said. "He is a physician also, the good Aunt's husband, and he understands. He will take her with him; and, if he did not, she would die; for, now that it is plain to her, how grievously she hath caused him to sorrow, her love is like a fever till she can make amends for all."

"Amends!" growled Dr. Macgowan, "that's just like a woman too. Amends! I'd like to know what amends there can be for such a scandal, such a disgrace: 'pon my word she must have been mad; that's the only way of accounting for it."

"It is not that there will be scandal," replied Father Antoine. "I am to marry them in the chapel, and there is no one in all the wide world, except to you and to me, that it will be known that they have been husband and wife before."

"Eh! What! Married again!" exclaimed Dr. Macgowan. "Well, that's like a woman too. Why, what damned nonsense! If she was ever his wife, she's his wife now, isn't she? I shouldn't think you'd lend yourself, Father Antoine, to any such transaction as that."

"Gently, gently!" replied Father Antoine: "rail not so at womankind. It is she who wishes to go with him at once; and who says as thou, that she is still his wife: but it is he who will not. He says that she hath for ten years borne a name other than his; that in her own country she hath been ten years mourned for as dead; that he hath by process of law, on account of her death, inherited and sold all the estate that she did own."

"Rich, was she rich!" interrupted Dr. Macgowan. "Well, 'pon my word, it's the most extraordinary thing I ever did hear of: never could have happened in England, sir, never!"

"I know not if it were a large estate," continued Father Antoine, "it would be no difference: if it had been millions she would have left it and come away. She was full of renunciation. Ah! but she must be beloved of the Virgin."

"So you are really going to marry them over again, are you?" broke in the impatient doctor.

"I have said that I would," replied Father Antoine, "and it is great joy to me: neither should it seem strange to you. Your church doth not recognize the sacrament of baptism, when it has been performed by unconsecrated hands of dissenters: you do rebaptize all converts from those sects. So our church does not recognize the sacrament of marriage, when performed by any one outside of its own priesthood. I shall with true gladness of heart administer the holy sacrament of marriage to these two so strangely separated, and so strangely brought together. They have borne ten years of penance for whatever of sin had gone before: the church will bless them now."

"Hem," said Dr. Macgowan, gruffly, unable to controvert the logic of Father Antoine's position in regard to the sacraments; "that is all right from your point of view: but what do they make of it; I don't suppose they admit that their first marriage was invalid, do they?"

Dr. Macgowan was in the worst of humors. He was about to lose a nurse who had been to him for ten years, like his right hand; and he was utterly discomfited and confused in all his confirmed impressions of her character, by these startling revelations of her history. He would not have been a Briton if these untoward combinations of events had not made him surly.

"Nay, nay!" said Father Antoine, placably. "Not so. It is only the husband; and he has but one thing to say: that she who was his wife died to him, to her country, to her friends, to the law. There is even in her village a beautiful and high monument of marble which sets forth all the recountal of her death. She would go back to that country with him, and confess to every man the thing she had done. She prayed him that he would take her. But he will not. He says it would be shame; and the name of his wife that died shall never be shamed. It is a narrow strait for a man who loves a woman. I cannot say that it is clear to me what my own will would be in such a case. I am much moved by each when I hear them talk of it. Ah, but she has the grand honesty! Thou shouldst have heard her cry out when he said that to confess all would be a shame.

"'Nay, nay!' cried she, 'to conceal is a shame.'

"'Ay!' replied her husband, 'but thou hast thought it no shame to conceal thyself for these ten years, and to lie about thy name.' He speaketh with a great anger to her at times, spite of his love.

"'Ah,' she answered him, in a voice which nigh set me to weeping: 'Ah, my husband, I did think it shame: but I bore it, for sake of my love to thee; and now that I know I was wrong, all the more do I long to confess all, both that and this, and to stand forgiven or unforgiven, as I may, clear in the eyes of all who ever knew me.'

"But he will not, and I have counselled her to pray him no more. For he has already endured heavy things at her hands; and, if this one thing be to her a grievous burden, all the more doth it show her love, if she accept it and bear it to the end."

"Well, well," said Dr. Macgowan, somewhat wearied with Father Antoine's sentiments and emotions, "I have lost the best nurse I ever had, or shall have. I'll say that much for her; but I can't help feeling that there was something wrong in her brain somewhere, which might have cropped out again any day. Most extraordinary! most extraordinary!" And Dr. Macgowan walked away with a certain lofty, indifferent air, which English people so well understand, of washing one's hands of matters generally.

There had, indeed, been a sore struggle between Hetty and her husband on this matter of their being remarried by Father Antoine. When Dr. Eben first said to her: "And now, what are we to do, Hetty?" she looked at him in an agony of terror and gasped:

"Why, Eben, there is only one thing for us to do; don't we belong to each other? don't you love me? don't you mean to take me home with you?"

"Would you go home with me, Hetty?" he asked emphatically; "go back to Welbury? let every man, woman, and child in the county, nay, in the State, know that all my grief for you had been worse than needless, that I had been a deserted husband for ten years, and that you had been living under an assumed name all that time? Would you do this?"

Hetty's face paled. "What else is there to do?" she said.

He continued:

"Could you bear to have your name, your father's name, my name, all dragged into notoriety, all tarnished by being linked with this monstrous tale of a woman who fled — for no reason whatever — from her home, friends, husband, and hid herself, and was found only by an accident?"

"Oh, Eben! spare me," moaned Hetty.

"I can't spare you now, Hetty," he answered. "You must look the thing in the face. I have been looking it in the face ever since the first hour in which I found you. What are we to do?"

"I will stay on here if you think it best," said Hetty. "If you will be happier so. Nobody need ever know that I am alive."

Doctor Eben threw his arms around her. "Leave you here! Why, Hetty, will you never understand that I love you?" he exclaimed; "love you, love you, would no more leave you than I would kill myself?"

"But what is there, then, that we can do?" asked Hetty.

"Be married again here, as if we had never been married! You under your new name," replied Doctor Eben rapidly.

Hetty's face expressed absolute horror. "We — you and I — married again! Why Eben, it would be a mockery," she exclaimed.

"Not so much a mockery," her husband retorted, "as every thing that I have done, and every thing that you have done for ten whole years."

"Oh, Eben! I don't think it would be right," cried Hetty. "It would be a lie."

"A lie!" ejaculated her husband, scornfully. Poor Hetty! The bitter harvest of her wrong deed was garnered for her, poured upon her head at every turn, by the pitilessness of events. Inexorable seasons, surer than any other seed-time and harvest, are those uncalendared seasons in which souls sow and reap with meek patience.

Hetty replied:

"I know I have lived, acted, told a lie, Eben. Don't taunt me with it. How can you, if you really believe all I have told you of the reasons which led me to it?"

"My Hetty," said Dr. Eben, "I don't taunt you with it. I do believe all you have told me. I do know that you did it for love of me, monstrous though it sounds to say so. But when you refuse now to do the only thing which seems to me possible to be done to repair the mistake, and say your reason for not doing it is that it would be a lie, how can I help pointing back to the long ten years' lie you have lived, acted, told? If your love for me bore you up through that lie, it can bear you up through this."

"Shall we never go home, Eben?" asked Hetty sadly.

"To Welbury? to New England? never!" replied her husband with a terrible emphasis. "Never will I take you there to draw down upon our heads all the intolerable shame, and gossiping talk which would follow. I tell you, Hetty, you are dead! I am shielding your name, the name of my dead wife! You don't seem to comprehend in the least that you have been dead for ten years. You talk as if it would be nothing more to explain your reappearance than if you had been away somewhere for a visit longer than you intended."

The longer they discussed the subject, the more vehement Dr. Eben grew, and the feebler grew Hetty's opposition. She could not gainsay his arguments. She had nothing to oppose to them, except her wifely instinct that the old bond and ceremony were by implication desecrated in assuming a second: "But what right have I to fall back on that old bond," thought poor Hetty, wringing her hands as the burden of her long, sad ten years' mistake weighed upon her.

Not until Hetty had yielded this point was there any real joy between her and her husband. As soon as it was yielded, his happiness began to grow and increase, like a plant in spring-time.

"Now you are mine again! Now we will be happy! Life and the world are before us!" he exclaimed.

"But where shall we live, Eben?" asked the practical Hetty.

"Live! live!" he cried, like a boy; "live anywhere, so that we live together!"

"There is always plenty to do, everywhere," said Hetty, reflectively: "we should not have to be idle."

Dr. Eben looked at her with mingled admiration and anger.

"Hetty!" he exclaimed, "I wish you'd leave off 'doing,' for a while. All our misery came of that. At any rate, don't ever try to 'do' any thing for me again as long as you live! I'll look out for my own happiness, the rest of the time, if you please."

His healing had begun when he could make an affectionate jest, like this; but healing would come far slower to Hetty than to him. Complete healing could perhaps never come. Remorse could never wholly be banished from her heart.

When it had once been settled that the marriage should take place, there seemed no reason for deferring it; no reason, except that Father Antoine's carnations were for some cause or other, not yet in full bloom, and both he and Marie were much discontented at their tardiness. However, the weather grew suddenly hot, with sharp showers in the afternoons, and both the carnations and the Ayrshire roses flowered out by scores every morning, until even Marie was satisfied there would be enough. There was no tint of Ayrshire rose which could not be found in Father Antoine's garden,— white, pink, deep red, purple: the bushes grew like trees, and made almost a thicket, along the western boundary of the garden. Early on the morning of Hetty's wedding, Marie carried heaped basketfuls of these roses, into the chapel, and covered the altar with them. Pierre Michaud, now a fine stalwart fellow of twenty-one, just married to that little sister of Jean Cochot, about whom he had once told so big a lie, had begged for the privilege of adorning the rest of the chapel. For two days, he and Jean, his brother-in-law, had worked in the forests, cutting down young trees of fir, balsam, and dogwood. The balsams were full of small cones of a brilliant purple color; and the dogwoods were waving with showy white flowers. Pierre set each tree in a box of moist earth, so that it looked as thriving and fresh as it had done in the forest; first, a fir, and then a dogwood, all the way from the door to the altar, reached the gay and fragrant wall. Great masses of Linnea vines, in full bloom, hung on the walls, and big vases of Father Antoine's carnations stood in the niches, with the wax saints. The delicate odor of the roses, the Linnea blossoms, and carnations, blended with the spicy scent of the firs, and made a fragrance as strong as if it had been distilled from centuries of summer. The villagers had been told by Father Antoine, that this stranger who was to marry their good "Tantibba," was one who had known and loved her for twenty years, and who had been seeking her vainly all these years that she had lived in St. Mary's. The tale struck a warm chord in the breasts of the affectionate and enthusiastic people. The whole village was in great joy, both for love of "Tantibba," and for the love of romance, so natural to the French heart. Every one who had a flower in blossom picked it, or brought the plant to place in the chapel. Every man, woman, and child in the town, dressed as for a *fête*, was in the chapel, and praying for "Tantibba," long before the hour for the ceremony. When Eben and Hetty entered the door, the fragrance, the waving flowers, the murmuring crowd, unnerved Hetty. She had not been prepared for this.

"Oh, Eben!" she whispered, and, halting for a moment, clung tighter to his arm. He turned a look of affectionate pride upon her, and, pressing her hand, led her on. Father Antoine's face glowed with loving satisfaction as he pronounced the words so solemn to him, so significant to them. As for Marie, she could hardly keep quiet on her knees: her silver necklace fairly rattled on her shoulders with her excitement.

"Ah, but she looks like an angel! may the saints keep her," she muttered; "but what will comfort M'sieur Antoine for the loss of her, when she is gone?"

After the ceremony was over, all the people walked with the bride and bridegroom to the inn, where the diligence was waiting in which they were to begin their journey; the same old vehicle in which Hetty had come ten years before alone to St. Mary's, and Doctor Eben had come a few weeks ago alone to St. Mary's, "not knowing the things which should befall him there."

It was an incongruous old vehicle for a wedding journey; and the flowers at the ancient horses' heads, and the knots of green at the cracked windows, would have made one laugh who had no interest in the meaning of the decorations. But it was the only four-wheeled vehicle in St. Mary's, and to these simple villagers' way of thinking, there was nothing unbecoming in Tantibba's going away in it with her husband.

"Farewell to thee! Farewell to thee! The saints keep thee, Bo Tantibba and thy husband! and thy husband!" rose from scores of voices as the diligence moved slowly away.

Dr. Macgowan, who had somewhat reluctantly persuaded himself to be present at the wedding, and had walked stiffly in the merry procession from the chapel to the inn, stood on the inn steps, and raised his hat in a dignified manner for a second. Father Antoine stood bareheaded by his side, waving a large white handkerchief, and trying to think only of Hetty's happiness, not at all of his own and the village's loss. As the shouts of the people continued to ring on the air, Dr. Macgowan turned slowly to Father Antoine.

"Most extraordinary scene!" he said, "'pon my word, most extraordinary scene; never could happen in England, sir, never." "Which is perfectly true; worse luck for England," Father Antoine might have replied; but did not. A few of the younger men and maidens ran for a short distance by the side of the diligence, and threw flowers into the windows.

"Thou wilt return! thou wilt return!" they cried. "Say thou wilt return!"

"Yes, God willing, I will return," answered Hetty, bending to the right and to the left, taking loving farewell looks of them all. "We will surely return." And as the last face disappeared from sight, and the last merry voice died away, she turned to her husband, and, laying her hand in his, said, "Why not, Eben? Will not that be our best home, our best happiness, to come back and live and die among these simple people?"

"Yes," answered Dr. Eben, "it will. Tantibba, we will come back."

And now is told all that I have to tell of the Strange History of Eben and Hetty Williams. If there be any who find the history incredible, I have for such a few words more.

First: I myself have seen, in the old graveyard at Welbury, the "beautiful and high monument of marble," of which Father Antoine spoke to Dr. Macgowan. It bears the following inscription:

"Sacred to the Memory
of
HENRIETTA GUNN,
Beloved Wife of Dr. Ebenezer Williams,
Who was drowned in Welbury Lake."

The dates, which I have my own reasons for not giving, come below; and also a verse of the Bible, which I will not quote.

Second: I myself was in Welbury when there was brought to the town by some traveller a copy of a Canadian newspaper, in which, among the marriages, appeared this one:

"In the parish of St. Mary's, Canada, W., by Rev. Antoine Ladeau, Mrs. Hibba Smailli to Dr. Ebenezer Williams."

The condition of Welbury, when this piece of news was fairly in circulation in the town, could be compared to nothing but the buzz of a beehive at swarming time. A letter which was received by the Littles, a few days later, from Dr. Williams himself, did not at first allay the buzzing. He wrote, simply: "You will be much surprised at the slip which I enclose" (it was the newspaper announcement of his marriage). "You can hardly be more surprised than I am myself; but the lady is one whom I knew and loved a great many years ago. We are going abroad, and shall probably remain there for some years. When I shall see Welbury again is very uncertain."

Thirdly: Since neither of these facts proves my "Strange History" true, I add one more.

I know Hetty Williams.

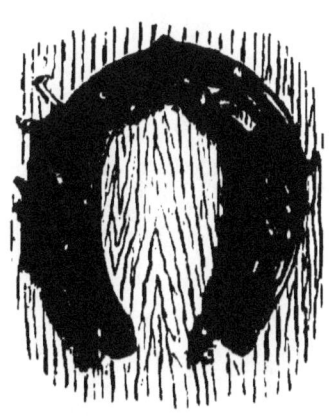

THE "NO NAME SERIES."

"IS THAT ALL?"

"In some respects, this is the best of the three volumes yet published of this series. For, though it does not go so deep as 'Mercy Philbrick,' nor deal in poetic fancies like 'Deirdrè,' it is better sustained on its own surface-level than either of those romances. It is not a romance at all in fact, but a pleasing sketch, somewhat too warmly colored, of New England social life in the well-bred circle of a small city, — say Hartford. The plot is simple and direct, and the story closes before it has time to become tiresome in any particular. . . . The book is all it professes to be, and something more, and will certainly be popular." — *Springfield Republican.*

"The new novel of the 'No Name Series' belongs of right to the class of stories which men and women take with them on vacation journeys. It has little plot, and what little there is is of the slightest kind. It is meant to be light and amusing, and is so in a high degree. The picture it gives of high life in a provincial city is very fine, and a spirit of bantering which runs through it makes it extremely piquant. As to the authorship it is idle to guess. We leave the solution of the question to the reader's own skill in reading riddles, and commend the anonymous book to his attention as one which will entertain him greatly, whether or not he can guess its origin." — *New York Evening Post.*

"'Is That All?' third in order of the conundrums at which the Messrs. Roberts have set the world a-guessing, perplexes conjecture in a greater degree than its predecessors. Its style recalls none of our better-known writers; and, in spite of the assurance of the publishers, we should be disposed to set it down as the work of a fresh hand, were it not for the practice and finish which it evinces. It is, to use its own words, a 'very *méringue* of a story,' light, crisp, delicately flavored; but, for all this sketchiness, it is full of real character and individuality. . . . There is a great deal of bright, natural conversation, some capital love-making, and both humor and good-humor in the pithy, half-sarcastic touches which glance here and there on the page like a smile out of quizzical, friendly eyes." — *Boston Transcript.*

"It is cleverly constructed in plot, and has the rare merit of seeming too short. The style is bright and animated, the characters are evidently drawn from life, and spiritedly drawn at that. The conversations are sparkling and witty, and the work is unmistakably from the hand of one thoroughly acquainted with the world and with good society. It is the best book of the series, thus far, though, as the author says, 'a very *méringue* of a story.' Its naturalness is not the least of its charms. We have been thoroughly delighted with it, and we assure our readers that they will derive equal pleasure and satisfaction from its perusal. The name of the author has not yet transpired, but we hazard the guess that it is a woman, — not owing to any effeminacy or weakness in the style, but from the fact that no one but a woman would write so saucily about the gentler sex. We advise everybody to read this clever little story." — *Saturday Gazette.*

In one volume, 16mo. Cloth. Gilt and red-lettered. $1.00.

Our publications are to be had of all Booksellers. When not to be found, send directly to

ROBERTS BROTHERS, Publishers, Boston.

THE "NO NAME SERIES."

KISMET. A Nile Novel.

Opinions, generous tributes to genius, by well-known authors whose names are anonymous.

"Well, I have read 'Kismet,' and it is certainly very remarkable. The story is interesting, — any well-told love story is, you know, — but the book itself is a great deal more so. Descriptively and sentimentally, — I use the word with entire respect, — it is, in spots, fairly exquisite. It seems to me all glowing and overflowing with what the French call *beauté du diable*. . . . The conversations are very clever, and the wit is often astonishingly like the wit of an accomplished man of the world. One thing which seems to me to show promise — great promise, if you will — for the future is that the author can not only reproduce the conversation of one brilliant man, but can make two men talk together as if they *were* men, — not women in manly clothes."

"It is a charming book. I have read it twice, and looked it over again, and I wish I had it all new to sit up with to-night. It is so fresh and sweet and innocent and joyous, the dialogue is so natural and bright, the characters so keenly edged, and the descriptions so poetic. I don't know when I have enjoyed any thing more, — never since I went sailing up the Nile with Harriet Martineau. . . . You must give the author love and greeting from one of the fraternity. The hand that gives us *this* pleasure will give us plenty more of an improving quality every year, I think."

"'Kismet' is indeed a delightful story, the best of the series undoubtedly."

"If 'Kismet' is the first work of a young lady, as reported, it shows a great gift of language, and powers of description and of insight into character and life quite uncommon. . . . Of the whole series so far, I think 'Mercy Philbrick's Choice' is the best, because it has, beside literary merit, some moral tone and vigor. Still there are capabilities in the writer of 'Kismet' even higher than in that of the writer of 'Mercy Philbrick's Choice.'"

"I liked it extremely. It is the best in the series so far, except in construction, in which 'Is That All?' slight as it is, seems to me superior. 'Kismet' is winning golden opinions everywhere. I have nothing but praises for it, and have nothing but praise to give it."

"I have read 'Kismet' once, and mean to read it again. It is thoroughly charming, and will be a success."

One volume, bound in cardinal red and black. Price $1.00.

Our publications are to be had of all booksellers. When not to be found, send directly to

ROBERTS BROTHERS, Publishers, Boston.

www.ingramcontent.com/pod-product-compliance
Lightning Source LLC
Chambersburg PA
CBHW032051230426
43672CB00009B/1558